The Dating Fast

The Dating Fast

40 Days to Reclaim Your Heart, Body, and Soul

KATHERINE BECKER

A Crossroad Book
The Crossroad Publishing Company
New York

The Crossroad Publishing Company
www.CrossroadPublishing.com

In continuation of our 200-year tradition of independent publishing, The Crossroad Publishing Company proudly offers a variety of books with strong, original voices and diverse perspectives. The viewpoints expressed in our books are not necessarily those of The Crossroad Publishing Company, any of its imprints or of its employees. No claims are made or responsibility assumed for any health or other benefit.

Printed in the United States of America.

The text of this book is set in Apollo

The display face is Helvetica

Project Management by
The Crossroad Publishing Company
John Jones

For this edition numerous people have shared their talents and ideas, and we gratefully acknowledge Katherine Becker, who has been most gracious during the course of our cooperation. We thank especially:

Cover design: Irene Archer   Text design: Web Fusion
Printing: Versa Press   Proofreading: Sylke Jackson

Message development, text development, package, and market positioning by
The Crossroad Publishing Company

Library of Congress Cataloging-in-Publication Data available from the publisher

ISBN 13: 978-0-8245-26924

Books published by The Crossroad Publishing Company may be purchased at special quantity discount rates for classes and institutional use. For information, please e-mail info@CrossroadPublishing.com

Table of Contents

Acknowledgments

In thanksgiving to God for constantly reminding me that I am His beloved daughter, and giving me the grace and courage to share my story. A special thanks to Father Luke Spannagel, Sr. Marie Benedicta of the Cross, Kayla Cvengros, and Erin MacDonald for their Christian witness, friendship, love, and prayers. Deepest thanks to my family for their support and love throughout my life, and encouragement to always dream big and follow my heart. Thank you to all of my besties and friends who have walked with me on my journey and continue to make my heart smile! Special thanks to Joanne Drake, Katie Knapp, and Dave Rafferty for helping me during the editing process. Sincerest gratitude to Matthew Kelly for believing in me and sending my manuscript to The Crossroad Publishing Company. Finally, many thanks to all those who have supported me and increased my capacity to love!

Prologue
You Are Loved

I love you. These three words can instill hope or incite fear. They can elicit great passion, or make you feel numb, cold, and bitter. What do these three words mean to you? Do they inspire hope and make your heart smile, or do they awaken anxiety and leave you feeling alone? Whatever these words mean to you, do you know that you are loved? Do you know Love?

You are loved. After all, you are a daughter of God. As His daughter you are united to His everlasting love and mercy. It is His love for you that led Him to the cross. His love for you is far greater than you could imagine. Though it will take a lifetime for you to begin to understand how much He loves you, may the 40-day dating fast help you discover genuine love: a love that flows from Christ, the source of all love; a love that stems from self-sacrifice and commitment; a love that is self-giving, not self-receiving; a love that permeates the depths of your heart and sustains you throughout life; a love whose capacity is infinite and is designed solely for the goodness of your soul. In short, may you discover a love that leads you to happiness now and for all eternity!

1

"What Will My Future Spouse Be Like?"

Like most women, I have dreamed about my future spouse for quite some time. Thoughts about our first date, first kiss, courtship, engagement, wedding, and family life have lingered in my mind since I was a little girl. When I was young, my childhood dream was to be a princess and to find my Prince Charming. All I wanted to be was a princess— nothing else. As a child, I remember sitting outside at night and looking at the stars, hoping and praying that it would be sooner rather than later that God would present me my husband. I prayed for God to unite us and bring us in union with one another. I would often find myself dreaming about my future spouse and wondering what he was doing at the present moment.

Throughout high school I did not date very many people. My senior year was the first time I was in a serious relationship. This young man taught me so much in the short time we were together. He had such a strong faith and was a devout man of God. He challenged me to grow deeper in my faith and helped me see the need to put Christ and others before myself. The relationship ended before I left for college, and the fact that it ended so quietly and suddenly confirmed that he was not the one. However, it was this relationship that opened my heart to love someone new, and I thank him for showing me how to develop an intimate relationship with another human.

Perhaps my heart was *too* open. My college years were filled with a series of bad and broken relationships— relationships I jumped too far into without fully thinking about our compatibility, and more importantly, God's plan. Like many young women I know, I was careless with my heart and in the end dated a number of wrong guys who broke my heart and left me with a lot of pain. At the same time, I cannot be too critical of these relationships because each person ended up teaching me something about myself, whether it was a personal trait, an interest, a hobby, or a characteristic. In addition, each of these relationships also showed me what I did *not* want. Towards the end of college, I finally recognized the need to be less careless with my heart, so I decided to take some time for personal reflection and growth. At that time, I had several decisions to make about what I was going to do after college, so it only seemed natural to focus on myself rather than seeking to find myself in someone else. It was during this period that I not only gained tremendous personal growth, but also saw my relationships with my friends start to thrive.

Promises to Myself

As I neared graduation from college, I decided that I wanted to start dating again. I knew that I needed to be more prudent with my heart and wiser about whom I entrusted it to in a dating relationship. So I vowed to myself that I would not get involved with anyone who was not Catholic, and I let other people know this as well. Although my relationship with God was far from being close or intimate, through His grace I began to realize the importance of my faith and the need to have faith-filled people in my life. I became certain that God wanted me to be with someone who shared my faith—someone who would help me grow closer to Him and not only pray with me but pray for me. I was gradually starting to take my faith more seriously when I met a young man, and because he was Catholic and attractive I immediately jumped into a relationship with him. Although the relationship started out well, it took a turn for the worse. Even though I knew that I needed to end the relationship, I stayed in it because I was not strong enough in my faith – I had already determined that he was "the one."

So many of us fall into the same trap. At some level, I knew that things needed to end because I was constantly unhappy, anxious, and upset, yet I was too afraid to lose him because I did not know who I was without him. In the end, I sacrificed a lot, including my relationship with God and myself. During the relationship, my prayer life and mass attendance decreased. I stopped spending time with friends and family. Overall, I was not prudent with my heart. Despite the pain of the break-up, I know it was the best thing that ever happened to me.

Finding a Guide

When our relationship ended, I was faced with a cold reality. I was so far away from God, my family and friends, and the strong Catholic woman I knew myself to have been just a year and a half earlier. I was alone and did not have the slightest clue where to turn. I felt unworthy and unloved.

By the grace of God, one night after mass, I had the courage to turn to a Catholic priest. He agreed to meet me for spiritual direction, and without knowing it at the time, this relationship would have a profound impact on my life.

I met with Father almost every week to talk about life, love, relationships, God, people, family, and friends. Because this was the first time I'd been in spiritual direction, it took a while for me to open up to him, but eventually things became easier. Our conversations flowed naturally, and I started to have hope again. I felt more comfortable sharing my life with him and knew that I was positively growing in my relationship with Christ. For the first time in a long time, I felt peace.

Although Father was helping me grow in my relationship with Christ, however, I still had a lot of residual pain in my heart from the previous break-up. I felt unworthy and unloved and harbored a lot of hatred towards my ex and his family and friends. After talking with a few friends, I decided that it would be best to go on a dating fast for three months to focus on my relationship with God and myself. One of my friends was a strong supporter of dating fasts, and it was her witness that solidified my decision to go on a fast. Although I had not dated anyone since my ex, I thought that it would be best for me to set aside time to focus solely on God and me. Little did I know the positive impact that these next few months would have on my personal journey! The dating fast would help me better understand my relationship with God and myself. Additionally, the dating fast would encourage me to concentrate on my relationships with friends and family and create stronger connections with them.

2

Your Longing for Intimacy

Like most of us, you long for intimacy, a deep connection of hearts. You yearn for that one person who will know you better than you know yourself: the one who can read your mind even though you don't say anything; the one who will listen when you need to vent; the one who will hold you, embrace you, and make you feel like you are cared for; the one who shows you that you matter and nothing else in the world is as important as you; the one who will accept you for who you are in the present moment and not judge you by who you once were or who you may become in the future. When you are with this person, time stands still.

People turn to many different things to discover this type of intimacy or to feel better when they don't have it: drugs, alcohol, sex, friends, or family. They believe that things and people can fill the empty void that lingers within their souls. While these things and people may provide you with a positive feeling or a sensation of happiness, it does not sustain itself. Eventually, the longing returns. Thus, all of these things really only serve as a distraction from the intimacy that your heart longs for—an intimacy that no human or earthly object can provide, an intimacy that can only come from God.

The harsh reality is that even the most compassionate people with the biggest hearts will fail you at some point in your life. We are human. We are fallible creatures prone to making mistakes. After all, we are descendants of Adam and

Eve, and thus we live in a sinful world. Does this mean that we are bad people with bad intentions? No. It means that we are human and we will fail in life. We will fail ourselves, we will fail those we love, and we will fail God. This is a fact of life and a bitter reality that we must learn to accept. However, accepting the reality of our failures does not mean surrendering or giving up on life. Our failures and limitations do not define who we are – they are guides to reveal what we must become. We must learn how to take these failures and mistakes and turn them into fruitful lessons that help us grow into the people we were meant to be.

3

What Is True Love?

It is important to understand what love is and know its Source. "Whoever does not love does not know God, because God is love. We love Him because He loved us first" (1 John 4:8; 19). We can't depend only on something or someone in this life. Yes, we are social creatures called to live in union with others, but we must never neglect our independence, our own unique free will, and the intimate relationship we have with Our Father. Only when we fully understand this unique free will and independence can we truly love others. You cannot give someone else something that you do not have, and this is especially true for love.

Today, society creates a difficult world for young women to obtain love. We live in a culture that promotes individuality and the need to exercise personal freedom. These liberties are often taken to the extreme and lead to negative consequences. Although we often hear that we need to isolate ourselves from others in order to achieve personal success and happiness, we must realize that ultimate happiness derives from living in communion with God and other people. Isolation, such as focusing solely on your career advancement, or becoming engrossed with a relationship that excludes other relationships in your life or neglects your prayer life, can be detrimental to your personal growth and health.

The need for mankind to live in communion with God and one another can be traced back to the creation of humans, when God created Eve to be in union with Adam. Adam lived in the beautiful garden alone. God recognized Adam's need for unity with another and thus created Eve to be Adam's wife. It was not until Eve entered Adam's life that he finally felt whole and complete. "The man said: this one, at last, is bone of my bones and flesh of my flesh; this one shall be called 'woman,' for out of 'her man' this one has been taken" (Genesis 2:23).

An important lesson should be learned from this story. Adam spent time working before he was joined in union with Eve. He spent time discovering himself and tending to the things in his life that needed to be addressed. He obediently followed God's orders and completed the work that he was given. But God knew that it was not good for man to be alone; He needed to create a suitable earthly partner for him. Therefore God cast a deep sleep upon Adam and took his rib to create Eve. This story of Adam and Eve suggests we must spend time alone discovering God and ourselves in order to truly live in union with another person. We must first tend to the necessary work within our own lives and hearts. We must first follow the example of Adam and cultivate and care for the garden that we live in, building on that relationship with Christ, before God presents us with a suitable spouse that He chooses.

4

Obtaining the Life You Have Always Dreamed Of

You may be wondering—*how can I obtain the life I have always dreamed of with a future spouse?* I will first tell you what *not* to do. Don't live the stereotypical life of a person in her 20s or 30s with no commitments, no obligations, and no burdens or strings of attachment. This is not love and will not help you discover true love. God says "you shall have no other gods before me." Therefore, we do need to have a commitment – to Him! And we must choose to place nothing above or before Him, including our relationships with other people and our lifestyles of freedom. You must learn to turn to Him, lean on Him, and love Him and only Him. It is through discovering or rediscovering Christ that you will obtain holiness, your heart will be filled with peace, and you will know what it means to love and be loved. In doing so, you will prepare yourself to carry out your vocation in complete joy—a joy that will sustain you throughout your life because you took the time to discover love and foster a relationship with Christ first.

But how do you get to this point of joyful love? Some people are more naturally graced with this gift and are fortunate to discover the answer early on. But most of us must discover it the hard the way. It usually takes some kind of struggle, challenge, or hurdle to make us humble enough to look beyond ourselves and turn to God. For myself, it was a series of crosses that led me into His arms. It was only after

I was able to look outside of myself, beyond my family, friends, and the rest of society, that I was able to recognize what it was I was being called to do. In the pages ahead, I hope to share with you my journey with Christ and provide you inspiration and hope for your own journey. May it give you peace knowing that someone else has once walked a similar road that you are being called to walk, not only surviving but thriving from the experience.

5

The Benefits of the Dating Fast

As I shared earlier, I went through a very difficult breakup a few years ago. The breakup was so painful because during the relationship, I took my eyes off of Christ and focused them on the guy. When the guy failed me and broke my heart, I was left empty and alone.

Thankfully, I was surrounded with many faith-filled people after the breakup, who helped me rediscover Christ and myself. These people challenged me to be more active in my faith life and devote time to building my relationship with Christ. Shortly after meeting with Father, I started to integrate prayer more frequently into my daily routine. Through prayer and the relationships that I was fostering with these faithful people, I came to realize that I needed to go on a dating fast. Even though I had not dated anyone since my ex and was not currently interested in anyone, I knew that I needed to set aside a period of time to foster a deep, intimate relationship with Christ and rediscover myself through His grace. Initially, I began my dating fast for five primary reasons. Many young women have a similar list:

a) heal from the pain that occurred,
b) work on the virtues of patience, hope, and trust,
c) deepen my relationship with God,
d) come to know and love myself—discover more deeply who I am and what I am called to do, and

e) forgive those who have hurt me and humbly ask for forgiveness for those that I have hurt.

Through the fast I learned a lot and grew in more ways than these five areas. This experience confirms that God truly does provide us with more than we ask. In order to obtain this grace, however, we must trust in His will and take the leap of faith.

Here are the seven blessings of the dating fast that stand out for me. Every woman has her own unique experience, but I include these here to give you an idea of the rich gifts Christ can bring to your life when you commit to making time for His love.

What the Dating Fast Taught Me

1. *The importance of forgiving others:* One of the primary reasons I went on this dating fast was to heal from the pain I carried from a previous dating relationship. So much hatred and vengeance remained in my heart that prevented me from being open and free to love. The dating fast taught me that no matter how much pain anyone may inflict upon me, I must forgive them. Forgiveness is liberating— it sets your heart free and enables you to love others. Without forgiveness, you will not be free to give and receive love.

2. *The importance of forgiving myself:* You must be willing to accept yourself for who you are. You will never be perfect; you will always make mistakes. Embrace your imperfections because they are a part of you. Do not let these imperfections define you or limit your desire to strive to be better. Learn from your mistakes—they are one of the greatest teachers

that you will ever receive. Do not question if God has forgiven you—He already has. Follow His example and forgive yourself. I realize that this step is not easy – I continue to struggle with it even now. We all have holes, but our weaknesses and imperfections are where God's light shines through.

3. *Patience:* Patience is a difficult virtue. We live in a society where we expect things to happen immediately. However, patience will teach you that all things come in due time. Those who wait will be rewarded. Just because *something* is not happening in the present moment does not mean that *nothing* is happening. In fact, when you practice patience, you can often discover the gift that is already right in front of you. Patience is a result of obedience to God and understanding that all things happen in God's perfect time. Since God is infinite and timeless, He knows our hearts' true desires and provides us with those gifts, fully knowing the greater picture of our lives and having our best interests in mind.

4. *Trust:* Life is challenging. Life is difficult. Some days you are terrified, and other days you may feel completely lost. However, you must have trust in the Lord. Trust that He will provide for you. Trust that He will fill your heart's desires. Trust in Him, for He will never let you go. Trust requires you to lean not on your own understanding but on His. In order to trust, you must surrender yourself to God and be open to His will. Psalm 37:4 says "Trust in the Lord, and He will give you the desires of your heart." A friend once suggested that the best way to read this passage is: He will give you the "true" desires of your heart. If you trust yourself to God, he will

begin to open your heart to what it truly desires, not what the world tells you it desires. God wants you to be happy for all eternity.

5. *Joy:* Many of my closest friends and family are filled with so much joy and happiness. I look at them and I see their hearts smiling, and in return it makes my heart smile. Their joy is contagious! It fills up the room with warmth, creating a presence of love and peace. True joy is always derived from God. It is He who places the people and things in our lives that bring us joy. To appreciate this, we must be open to that joy but never confuse it with the ultimate joy we receive when we are in union with God.

6. **The things that make me unique:** All of us have our own unique qualities. What in your life makes you unique? I love cooking, especially for small groups of people. I not only love preparing the meal but being able to share that meal with others. Some of my best memories are dinner dates (especially when there are avocados!). I love peanut butter M&Ms. I love biking and running. I love being outdoors. I love having long, deep conversations with people. I love watching college football games (especially the Hawkeyes and the Illini). I love listening to music, especially songs by Mark Schultz. I love working with children. I love long walks. I love wine— especially red wines! And how could I forget? I love to dance! The list could go on. Throughout the dating fast, I was opening myself up to my family and friends, who helped me rediscover the things in my life that bring me happiness and make me unique.

The dating fast will help you discover what makes you unique. As 1 Corinthians 12 discusses, there is one body, but many parts. We are each created as individuals. By being true to ourselves, we discover what contribution we can make to the Kingdom, and we grow toward our sanctification and ultimate happiness.

7. *The ability to love myself:* Psalm 46:10 states "Be still and know that I am God." It was through quiet prayer and silence that I started to understand that I am a woman of faith. I can be strong. I desire to love and be loved. My happiest times are when I am able to do things for other people. I love being around my friends because each of them brings out the best in me. Each person teaches me something about life. My friends challenge me to pursue excellence every day. They teach me to be selfless and to think about others first. They show me how to love and be loved. They truly love me for who I am. They teach me to turn to prayer in times of need. They inspire me and give me hope—hope that I am living the life I am called to live, hope that I will one day have the opportunity to be a wife and a mother, to earn my Ph.D., to complete my "bucket list" and leave the world a better place. I look at their lives and I see God's presence working within each of them, and it gives me hope that He is working in mine as well.

I offer these personal reflections as an example. I encourage you to spend some time creating your own list of goals that you hope to achieve on the dating fast. Spend time in prayer talking to God about these goals and listen to Him to see if there is anything that He wants you to discover. Then use the following page to write down what you wish to achieve and experience during your 40 days.

My Goals for the Dating Fast

- Become more of a woman after God.

- Realign my morals + values.

- Strengthen my purity

- Fall in love with God

- Put God first

- Be more compassimate + Joyful.

6

Accepting the Ultimate Challenge

All women should pursue a dating fast at some point during their single life, especially if they desire the vocation of marriage. The idea of a dating fast may seem odd. You might wonder: if you desire to be in a serious relationship with someone, how can stepping away from the dating scene actually make you better at finding the person you desire to spend your life with? What about "putting yourself out there," playing the field and meeting as many people as possible in order to find "the one"?

My answer to this is simple. *You cannot find someone until you know what you're looking for.* Even if you know what qualities you want in a future spouse, you must first know God in order to know love and what it means for your life. God will heal you from past pain during your dating fast. Even if there is not great pain, He will provide you with a greater awareness and understanding of what type of man He wants you to marry. He will give you a greater knowledge of yourself and your heart and lead you on the path to seeking that future marriage relationship.

If you truly desire to be in a committed relationship and enter into a fruitful marriage, you must first take time for yourself and go on a dating fast. Marriage can be described as a love dare that you carry out with your spouse. But in order to enter into any love dare with another individual, you must first dare to love—you must dare to love God and yourself, to understand that the unconditional *agape* love required for a thriving marriage is a rare gem solely residing in the depths of your soul. Prayer, quiet reflection, solitude, fasting, family, friendships, the sacraments, time, and journaling will help you discover this love. So I dare you to love yourself and trust your heart to the One who is Love and the only One who can reveal your true worth.

This is not an easy journey to accept. As you get older, you may start to feel alone and even desperate, especially if many people around you are in committed relationships. Your own family may also be pressuring you to find that special someone "before it's too late." You may witness friends getting married and starting to have children. If this is something that you desire, a sense of longing may permeate your heart and make you yearn for their life. Remember that coveting is a sin. If you start to feel this longing and desire, you have a choice—you can fixate on what is out of your control and what you do not have, or you can focus on what you do have. I encourage you to place total trust in God: trust that He will provide for you at His perfect time. After all, He is the one who places the desires in your heart, including that desire for a spouse and children. Since He places those desires in your heart, He will provide for you.

God knows exactly where you are in your life because he has placed you there. If you are single, He knows you are single. You are single for a reason—because God has not led you to the opportunity to be married yet. Believe that once you do get married, it will be due to His perfect timing. This time of trust, prayer, and quiet self-reflection during the dating fast will move beyond relationships and lead you to ask the bigger questions in life: *What are your goals? What are your dreams? What are your aspirations? What makes your heart smile? And what is fueling these desires?* These questions take a considerable amount of time and effort to answer honestly. They require you to be courageous and honest with yourself and to listen to Christ speak to you within the depths of your heart. You must open your heart and see yourself for all that you are and all that God has created you to become.

Finally, bear in mind that being single offers you a great opportunity – <u>time</u>! Instead of looking back with regret later, take advantage of this time while you have it.

God tells us in James 1:5–8, *"If you need wisdom—if you want to know what God wants you to do—ask Him, and He will gladly tell you. He will not resent your asking. But when you ask Him, be sure that you <u>really expect Him to answer</u>, for a doubtful mind is as unsettled as a wave of the sea that is driven and tossed by the wind. People like that should not expect to receive anything from the Lord. They can't make up their minds. They waver back and forth in everything they do."*

Ask the Lord, and listen. Take time during the dating fast to develop and strengthen an intimate relationship and friendship with God, your Father. Spend time on the dating fast rediscovering God, and you will rediscover yourself and have more fruitful relationships. The dating fast will provide you with three important graces: self-reflection that leads to greater self-awareness, healing, and growth. If you take this journey seriously, you will receive each of these blessings. Make sure that you concentrate on each element, so that you not only heal, but also grow. Do not merely become *aware of* God's will – cooperate with it. You are about to embark on an incredible journey that will change the rest of your life if you let yourself fall in love with God. Enjoy the ride!

We now begin the practical guide to the 40-day dating fast. Each day includes a scripture passage, meditation, and "dare" that centers around a particular theme. I encourage you to spend time each morning going through the reading for that day so that you can try to integrate the dare into your daily routine. Each reflection and scripture passage is short, so that even those of you who are busy can find time for reading, prayer, and reflection with God. If you make this dating fast a priority and take 5 to 10 minutes each morning to begin your day in prayer, I am positive that you will receive many blessings and graces on this fast.

> "I am the way, the truth, and the life. No one can come to the Father except through Me."; "Look! Here I stand at the door and knock. If you hear me calling and open the door, I will come in, and we will share a meal as friends."
>
> (John 14:6; Revelation 3:20)

True love comes from God and God alone

1 Corinthians 4–8; 13 "Love is patient, love is kind. It is not jealous, [love] is not pompous, it is not inflated, it is not rude, it does not seek its own interests, it is not quick-tempered, it does not brood over injury, it does not rejoice over wrongdoing but rejoices with the truth. It bears all things, believes all things, hopes all things, and endures all things. Love never fails."; "So faith, hope, love remain, these three; but the greatest of these is love."

To discover love on your dating fast, you must first discover the author of love. Know that you are worthy and loved because God loved you first. God tells us, "I have loved you even before you were born and will continue to love you for all eternity. I gave my life so that you may live. Follow me. Follow my example of self-sacrifice and commitment. This is the only kind of love that is genuine and real. This kind of love is the love I have for you and the love I want you to have for all eternity." God's love for us is infinite and began before we were born. God sent Jesus to show the world the infinite capacity of His love. Jesus' example shows us that God loves us so much that He would allow His only son to die on the cross for our sins.

If we follow the example of Jesus, we must try to love people with the same regard. When you love someone in a

Christlike way, you wish that person eternity. You set aside your own feelings and emotions for the best interest of the other person. You love the person for who they are and not what they do or fail to do. You see each person as God would see them, as a beautiful son or daughter of Christ. Understanding this type of love will help you better know God, who is the Source of Love. True love comes from God and God alone, and as we understand God we will understand love. Keep God at the center of your life and love Him first. Let His love pour out onto all the areas of your life.

St. Teresa of Avila beautifully describes genuine love:

> For love consists not in the extent of our happiness, but in the firmness in our determination to try to please God in everything and to endeavor in all possible ways not to offend Him, and to ask Him ever to advance the honor and glory of His Son and the growth of the Catholic Church.

DARE: Meditate on 1 Corinthians 13, above. What does God say love is? What does this mean to you? How is this similar to or different from your present understanding of love? Since we understand that God is love, reread the Bible passage and replace the word love with God. Imagine that God is revealing to you who He is. How does this make you feel? Now reread the passage a third time and replace the word love with your name. As you read this passage with your name, think about how you can become more Christlike, more like pure love. Imagine God reading this to you and telling you that this is who He made you to be. Now set goals to purify your love on this fast. For instance, set aside time each day to sit in silence and allow God to show you His love.

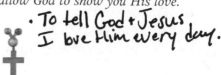
- To tell God + Jesus I love Him every day.

We are made for love

1 Corinthians 1–3 "If I speak in human and angelic tongues but do not have love, I am a resounding gong or a clashing cymbal. And if I have the gift of prophecy and comprehend all mysteries and all knowledge; if I have all faith so as to move mountains but do not have love, I am nothing. If I give away everything I own, and if I hand my body over so that I may boast but do not have love, I gain nothing."

We are all made out of love for love. Love is the one universal language that all humans share. We all desire to love and be loved. Jesus' life on earth was to teach us how to love better. The two great commandments reveal the process of love. 1) You shall love the Lord, your God, and 2) You shall love your neighbor as yourself. Note the order of the commandments. *First* love God and *then* love neighbor with the love that you have for yourself. This chain of love is a key for better understanding how to love. We must love God first, to learn to love ourselves, and then we must share that love with others. We must understand Love from its Source in order to share that love with those around us.

[handwritten margin note: implying we must love Jesus to show neighbors His love]

[handwritten annotation: Source → Jesus]

The dating fast allows you to focus on God, which in turn will give you the opportunity to focus on Love. During the fast you will have the opportunity to fill up your cup with love so you can share that love with others. You will

[handwritten note at bottom: love God → You → Your neighbor.]

learn that love is not just a feeling or flighty emotion. Love is a choice. It involves a sacrifice to place the needs and desires of another person's heart above your own. When you truly love another person, your heart becomes vulnerable in hope to receive the vulnerability of another person's heart. God is one person whose heart you will receive in return if you give Him yours. Learn from the One who is Love, the one who sent His only Son to teach us how to love others. By learning to love God, you will learn to love yourself. This love will overflow into all areas of your life, including your relationships with others. How much love you give God is the best indicator of your capacity to love your future spouse and children. Love Christ first, and He will purify your love for other people.

DARE: Write a love letter to God. How do you love Him already? In what ways would you like to love Him more deeply?

Practicing patience

Psalm 27:14 "Wait patiently for the Lord. Be brave and courageous. Yes, wait patiently for the Lord."

Patience. So many people try to obtain this virtue, yet few do so because they lack the patience! The dating fast will teach you to be patient because it forces you to slow down your life, stop focusing on men and other things, and place your trust in God. Throughout the fast, you will have the opportunity to exhibit patience by concentrating on the inner workings of your heart. If you spend time in silence and prayer, you will begin to recognize Christ's presence within your life.

Your awareness of Christ's presence will not only foster a sense of peace, but you will also recognize more clarity and Truth. There is a Truth that stems from certitude of the heart and the mind. This certitude does not mean that you never have any doubts. After all, you can never be 100% certain of anything except for the dogmas of the Church. The certitude that I reference, however, is a moral certitude, or rather a moral compass. This moral compass is led by both the mind and the heart and produces a sense of peace that cannot be described and is only known by those who have experienced it. When you have reached this level of certainty, you will understand this Truth.

Patience is a vital pillar of the fast. You must learn to clear your mind of all your worries, anxieties, fears, frustrations, lists, and daily activities in order to truly relax and exhibit patience. If this quiet stillness is unfamiliar to you and you need something to concentrate on, then meditate on the Biblical phrase, "God is love and all who live in God live in Love." Just continue to repeat that phrase in your mind. Do not get too caught up in its meaning, but rather use this phrase to relax your mind and clear your head of unnecessary thoughts that prevent you from being in the quiet and stillness where God resides and speaks. Give yourself enough time to listen. Be patient with yourself and God. Do not place too many restrictions or limitations on your relationship with Him. If you are more of a "doer," then slow down your life and just be. While we are meant to act, we are also meant to be present in this world and be patient.

DARE: Spend 15 minutes in silence. Do not keep your eye on the clock, but rather close your eyes, open your mind, and just be still. If you start to think about things, start over. You must learn to train your body to be still to hear God's voice. Remember that God's voice lies within the deep recesses of your soul, and you must be still and silent to hear His voice. As Psalm 46:10 states, "Be still and know that I am God."

"God is love + all who live in God live in love."

Divine surrender

John 12: 46–47 "I came into the world as light, so that everyone who believes in me might not remain in darkness. And if anyone hears my words and does not observe them, I do not condemn him, for I did not come to condemn the world but to save the world."

Henry David Thoreau once said "most men lead lives of quiet desperation and go to the grave with the song still in them." Thoreau realized that many people have their priorities confused and clutter their lives with too many things. The majority of people search for happiness in all of the wrong places. Look around you, and you will realize how many people fill their lives with things or appointments to keep themselves busy. They live minute-to-minute and day-to-day, struggling to make it to the following week. They desperately seek fulfillment and peace, but their present lifestyles prevent them from obtaining it. At the end of the day, they barely survive.

Thoreau hints at an essential concept—surrender. We must free ourselves from our present culture's demands in order to avoid living a life of quiet desperation. By freeing ourselves from the things and people that weigh us down, we can be open to God. It is important to know God and feel His presence in your heart. Surrender to God, and He will show you that the Holy Spirit is present in every moment of your life.

It can be scary handing everything over to God. Many people fear that God will take everything they desire and ask them to do something they do not want. This way of thinking is false, especially when you understand that God is love. Since God is Love, and love is linked to all of the virtues (such as faith, hope, and justice), surrendering to God will allow you to attain peace and fulfillment. In addition, God gives us free will to make the choice to surrender. We have the choice to survive or thrive in life. God will never force us to do anything. Remember that God is the One who places the desires deep within your heart. If you are honest with yourself, you will realize that He is the only person who can fulfill your desires and lead you to a life of happiness on this earth. God cannot fill what is already full—He can only fill where there is space. Therefore, empty your life of all the worldly clutter and surrender your life to God. Throughout your dating fast, God must increase while you decrease, as the Bible teaches us. It is only when you surrender that you will begin to obtain happiness in this life.

DARE: Read the gospel passage of the Samaritan woman (John 4:3–42) and reflect on Jesus as a man who is seeking your own heart. What type of man was Jesus? What type of man might he be calling you into marriage with in order to help you spend eternity with God the Father? Generate a list of attributes and qualities for the man you want to marry, using Jesus as the ideal man. Once you have generated a substantial list, after the dating fast, I challenge you to turn to the list whenever you meet potential suitors, using it as a guide to understand if the man you are spending time with and dating embodies the qualities of the man God would want you to marry.

Sacrifice and fasting

Matthew 6:16–18 "When you fast, do not look gloomy like the hypocrites. They neglect their appearance, so that they may appear to others to be fasting. Amen, I say to you, they have received their reward. But when you fast, anoint your head and wash your face, so that you may not appear to be fasting, except to your Father who is hidden. And your Father who sees what is hidden will repay you."

Fasting is something most Catholics do not think about except during Lent. Even when Catholics do think about it, it's usually in terms of food. While food is one item we can abstain from, though, there are other elements of our lives that demand fasting. For instance, if you spend a lot of time in front of the TV, on the Internet, or listening to your iPod, it may be good to fast from these items every now and then in order to spend more time with God, yourself, or the other relationships in your life. Fasting helps free you from any daily pleasures that bind and control your life. In addition, it creates a hunger that will make you more humble and open to recognizing the daily graces God bestows in your life.

When we fast, we offer up our actions as a sacrifice in order to build up ourselves. Consequently, when we fast from TV, we sacrifice the time that we would spend watching a show in order to use that time differently. When we fast from the distractions in our lives, that time can be spent in fruitful actions—prayer with God, helping a friend, journaling, or exercising.

Jesus offers the best example of fasting and sacrifice. Jesus went into the desert for 40 days and fasted before His death and resurrection. This fast created a physical and spiritual hunger that prepared Him for His passion and death as a sacrifice for our sins. Similarly, we must enter the desert of our own lives in order to hear God's voice and prepare ourselves for whatever God is calling us to do. When fasting is offered as a sacrifice with a seeking heart, God will bring forth answers and graces. During the dating fast, you must ask God to help you understand the areas in your life that need fasting. What items or experiences can you sacrifice for the betterment of God, others, and yourself? This sacrificial offering will create a hunger that should compel you to always strive for holiness. No matter how threatening it may seem, self-sacrifice is not a total sacrifice of your identity. In fact, it will help you discover your identity, as you use yourself as an instrument to serve God and others.

DARE: Spend today fasting from something that you enjoy. For instance, you could fast on only bread and water for the entire day and offer up your hunger for all of those who are less fortunate. Another option may be to not listen to music for the whole day and spend that time in silent prayer. Do not complain—this will take away from the purity of your sacrifice. Remember the Bible passage from Romans 5:3–5: "We also glory in our sufferings, because we know that suffering produces perseverance; perseverance, character; and character, hope. And hope does not put us to shame, because God's love has been poured into our hearts through the Holy Spirit, who has been given to us."

6

Embracing the present moment

Psalm 23:1–6 "The Lord is my shepherd; there is nothing I lack. In green pastures you let me graze; to safe waters you lead me; you restore my strength. You guide me along the right path for the sake of your name. Even when I walk through a dark valley, I fear no harm for you are at my side; your rod and staff give me courage. You set a table before me as my enemies watch; You anoint my head with oil; my cup overflows. Only goodness and love will pursue me all the days of my life; I will dwell in the house of the Lord for years to come."

Embrace the elements of your present life. When you learn to accept life for what it is at the present moment, not what it was in your past or what you hope it will be in the future, the rest of your life will begin to fall into place. By accepting the present moment, you will be forced to focus on others and not on the things that are lacking in your own life, such as a spouse or children. Your present life builds a foundation for what is to come next. So if you desire a serious dating relationship or a future marriage and children, you must take the necessary steps to prepare yourself for that vocation. You must learn to love and serve God first, then yourself, so that you are able to share that love with your future spouse and children. You cannot give something to someone that you do not have for yourself. Therefore, if you struggle with loving God or yourself, you will not be able to truly love another human being. Through prayer, ask God for the graces needed to love Him. You must fill up your cup with the graces that God has and wants to bestow upon you in order to share those graces with your future spouse and children.

While you are on the dating fast, take one day at a time. Concentrate on the things that occur during that day instead of focusing on the past or distant future. If you are someone who likes to plan things out with schedules and detailed outlines, make a special point to try to relax during these 40 days. Your goal on this fast should be to pray for graces to properly heal and grow in the areas of your life that need healing and growth. Set this as your goal, and leave the details and process up to God. Know that He wants what is best for you and will take care of your future. Your spiritual life is a house that you live in every day, one you invite all of your relationships into. Cultivate and tend to your house first before you let guests inside. Enjoy the present moment. Cultivate the relationships currently in your life, whether with family, friends, or coworkers. Because you are single, God is allowing you to have the time to love these individuals in unique and special ways that will only become more challenging when you are married or have a family. Enjoy this blessing of the single life by learning how to love these people more richly.

DARE: Go for a 20-minute walk outside alone. Do not bring any headphones or other distractions. If you live in an area with trees and quiet outdoors, simply enjoy nature's beauty and listen to the sounds and noises of nature and your environment. If you live in a more urban area, try to find a park or quiet area outside where you can be alone. Take the time to notice the city noises and embrace the sights and sounds of your surroundings. Spend the time outside talking to God. Ask Him to bestow His grace upon you now and always.

Created in God's image

Genesis 1:27 "God created man in his image, in the divine image he created him; male and female he created them."

On the fast it is important to understand and know who you are—*God's beautiful daughter*. A greater understanding of yourself will help reveal the things you need to recognize and receive on this fast. So start at the beginning and know that even before you were born, God had a plan for you and decided to create you in His divine image and likeness. Contemplate what it means to be created in the image and likeness of God. You are God's beautiful and special daughter. Every day He desires to be present with you and have you live with Him.

Throughout your life, you have made a series of choices. Reflect on these decisions and how they have led you to the present moment. Your past will help reveal where you are presently, and this understanding will guide your choices on how to carry out your future. Without honesty you will only be creating a façade and distracting yourself from the Truth, so be honest with yourself as you begin to uncover your identity. If at times this seems difficult, keep in mind that you will be discovering your identity as a beloved daughter of God.

DARE: Think about who you are at this present moment. How would you describe yourself? Start with the most basic things and be sure to include more deep aspects of your identity. What do you love? What makes you unique? What makes your heart smile? What things would God say are your best attributes? Also reflect on your not-so-good attributes. Know that everything you write, the good, the bad, and the ugly, is a part of you. Think about how you will begin to accept yourself. Make sure that you don't focus on the negative, for God would want you to know that you are beautiful, loved, and special.

Being aware of the internal reality

Song of Songs 8:6B "Set me as a seal on your heart, as a seal on your arm; For stern as death is love, relentless as the nether world is devotion; its flames are a blazing fire."

The future is an external expression of our internal realities. Simply put, this expression means that your future is often dependent on the emotional and psychological state within you.

When I was a little girl, my dad always told me that if I wanted to win a sporting competition, ace an exam, or perform well, I had to go into the experience with a positive mindset. He told me that if I did not think that I was going to succeed, I wouldn't—a self-fulfilling prophecy would occur. This is why mental preparation is a necessary precursor to any event. My dad not only emphasized the need for me to do this, but he also told me how mental preparation always helped him succeed on his examinations in medical school and residency. He shared stories with me about how he would play the same song before every exam (his choice was "Under Pressure" by David Bowie and Queen). This song raised his adrenaline and prepared him mentally and psychologically for the exam. I'm sure you and other people you know have similar rituals you perform before starting exams, competitions, events, meetings, or interviews. Many people recognize the importance of mental preparation.

In addition to helping you prepare for major events or competitions, mental preparation is also an important part of your personal journey. As Christians, we also note the significance of other kinds of preparation, including spiritual and emotional. If you are not mentally, psychologically, emotionally, or spiritually at peace, personal interior reflection is demanded. If you happen to be unhappy with your present state in life, stop and reflect on where you are interiorly. How is your relationship with Christ? Would you consider Him a true friend, or is He merely someone you pray to when you need something? Establishing a close and intimate relationship with Christ is important not only to discover Him, but also to discover *you*. As you start to discover Him more clearly, you will start to learn more about yourself. After all, we believe that He is our Creator, so if you want answers, travel the road of self-discovery and ask the One who made you.

Remember that it is important not just to ask God for things but also to listen. Effective listening requires silence and stillness. In most cases, God's voice is not a booming trumpet or a loud voice like it was with Abraham in the Old Testament. God is typically a gentle stillness and peace that resides within the depths of your soul. Often, we must be patient, still, and quiet in order to hear His voice.

It has been said that "a woman's heart should be so hidden in God that a man has to seek Him just to find her." This statement reveals the way in which men must discover women, and also hints at the way that a woman must discover herself. In order to protect your heart, learn about yourself, and discover true, genuine love in its most pure form. This must first occur by establishing a close and intimate relationship with Christ. Your relationship with Him supersedes all other relationships in your life and should be your first priority. It is not until you establish a relationship with Christ that you are truly ready to enter into a serious dating relationship, much less marriage.

Christ should always be your first priority. Your focus should be solely on Him. The men who come into your life and want to establish an intimate relationship with you must know God and be eager to continually discover God in order to find you. Furthermore, they must help bring you closer to God and challenge you in ways that lead you to Him.

DARE: Pray the rosary and meditate on your relationship with God. (See the end of this book for a guide on how to pray the rosary.) Even if you are not very familiar with the rosary, you can use this opportunity to grow in your understanding of this form of prayer.

Finding the balance between head and heart

Colossians 3:14–15 "And over all these put on love, that is, the bond of perfection. And let the peace of Christ control your hearts, the peace into which you were also called in one body. And be thankful."

Throughout your fast, your feelings about different things will change, but what should not change are your reasons, your faith, and your love. Therefore, all decisions must be made with both your head and heart. Remember, though, that in most matters the heart should be subordinate to the head since the heart's sole desire and purpose is to love and be loved. The heart on its own cannot discern which object of love is the best. Relying only on your heart may lead you astray. The heart can experience a fleeting emotion tied only to a situation or moment, and once that situation is removed the emotion subsides. Therefore, particularly during the dating fast, when your heart is healing, do not make decisions in the heat of the moment.

You cannot rely solely on the mind, either. This may cause you to be too analytical and prevent you from feeling the desires that burn deep within your soul. This is why there must be a balance between your mind and heart. The mind sees what the heart cannot feel, while the heart feels what the mind cannot see. Let your head influence your heart, and let your heart influence your head. Only time in quiet prayer and reflection will enable you to understand what this balance means for you. During your fast, seek to obtain knowledge of the heart that creates clarity and peace. This type of peace is more of a knowing than a feeling, but it is deeper than merely knowing a fact – it is wisdom. All future choices in your life should be made with the wisdom of the head and heart.

DARE: Journal about a time when your heart was leading you in a particular direction that later proved to be the wrong one. Reflect on your emotions throughout that experience. What did the heart feel? How might the situation have turned out differently if the head had been involved as well?

Reflecting on the past creates hope for the future

Luke 15:31–32 "He said to him, 'My son, you are here with me always; everything I have is yours. But now we must celebrate and rejoice, because your brother was dead and has come to life again; he was lost and has been found.'"

Many of us know the expression "every saint has a past, every sinner has a future." Regardless of what our pasts include, they can lead us to sainthood and a hopeful future with God. In the story of the prodigal son (Luke 15:11–32), Jesus reveals that some individuals' pasts may not be the most holy! Each soul, however, has the potential for His mercy and for the ability to receive God's love, both on this earth and in heaven. When the prodigal son returned home, the Father was filled with joy and threw a special feast upon his return. Not once does the story mention the Father's disappointment or frustration. God is a merciful Father who is passionately in love with us and patiently waits with open arms, hoping that we choose Him and come home to Him, just like the younger son in the story of the prodigal son. He loves us even when we do not love Him.

The story of Peter in the gospels also reveals the infinite nature of God's love. As a disciple of Christ, Peter loved God very much. At the time of Jesus' greatest need, however, when Jesus was arrested and crucified, Peter abandoned Christ and went so far as to deny Him three times. Even so, Jesus forgave Peter and continued to love Him. He even made Peter the first Pope, the rock of the Catholic Church. Jesus showed Peter God's mercy and love. While our pasts shape the journey that we have traveled, they do not define or constrain our present or future. God gives us free will, and this will provides us with hope for a future with Him, whatever our pasts may be.

Even though we can overcome our past, there is still much that it can teach us. Through prayer and quiet reflection, use the dating fast to think about your childhood and family life. As you grew up, what were your dreams and aspirations? How did you spend your childhood and youth? How did you change throughout the course of your life? Do you have any past regrets? Through reflecting on your past, what have you learned about yourself? Do certain experiences in your past characterize your present behaviors or attitudes? How can you use your past as a lesson to seek a future with God?

Remember that no past is unworthy of God's love. If you ever begin to question your own self-worth and ability to receive God's love, open a Bible and read about the types of sinners Christ loved. There are stories of sinners with ugly, horrible pasts. These sinners were thieves, adulterers, liars, and prostitutes. They were often outcasts from society because of the horrible crimes they had committed against themselves and others. Yet Jesus came to be with these sinners, show them their self-worth, give them hope, and tell them that they are loved. God loves you no matter what, and nothing you do can change His love for you. He desires your future to be bigger than your past.

DARE: Ask a family member or friend to share their favorite memory of you. Have a conversation about this experience. What positive qualities about you did they remember from the experience? Bask in the love being shared between the two of you.

Remembering childhood

Isaiah 127:3–4 "Children too are a gift from the Lord, the fruit of the womb, a reward. Like arrows in the hand of a warrior are the children born in one's youth."

Children are wonderful gifts from God. Innocence, purity, trust, obedience, and honesty are just a few of the virtues God gives all children. Unfortunately, as we grow up, these virtues often become tainted or stripped away entirely. The fear and uncertainty that plague adulthood is rarely a concern for most children. This is because of their innocence, purity, and total dependence on the individuals who care for them. If you spend time with a child or reflect upon your own childhood, you may discover who God is and what He is calling you to do.

God calls each of us to be more childlike. Since we are called to be more childlike, why does God allow us to grow up in this world? In part, we must grow up in order to acquire the adult virtue of wisdom and understand the essence of free will and choice in love; in part, however, we need to maintain our childhood virtues throughout our lives.

While I was at mass one day I realized the beauty of childhood and why God wants us to be more childlike. I was kneeling after communion and looked over to see the priest offer communion to a mother and bless the child she was holding. The girl stuck out her hand and said "Mommy, I want that." The priest simply smiled and gave her a blessing. As the mother walked away the child started to shout "Mommy, I want that" and eventually began to cry. It dawned on me that the mentality of this little girl, her desire for Christ, her innocence and purity in wanting the Eucharist, is how we should all approach Christ daily, but especially when we receive the Eucharist at mass. Recapturing that childlike innocence and dependence will bring you closer to God.

DARE: Look at pictures of yourself when you were younger and reflect on what you were like as a child. What were your dreams, and why? How has your relationship with God changed over the years? In what ways did you trust God more than you do today?

Dealing with pain

Matthew 11:28–30 "Come to me, all of you who are weary and carry heavy burdens, and I will give you rest. Take my yoke upon you. Let me teach you, because I am humble and gentle, and you will find rest for your souls. For my yoke fits perfectly, and the burden I give you is light."

We all have pain and suffering in our lives. While love is the universal language we all speak, pain is the universal struggle we all experience. On this earth, we will all battle with pain – it is inevitable. The difference lies in what we do with that pain. We are given a choice. We can bottle up the pain and try to suppress it, or we can face it head-on and look for a way to not let it control our lives. This is much easier said than done, especially if the pain is from an experience where you felt out of control in a situation initiated by someone else. The harsh reality about life is that people will cause us pain, and often the people closest to us will leave us with the most pain. This is because we have shared with them a piece of our heart, so when they hurt, disappoint, or leave us, the pain penetrates to the deepest recesses of our heart.

The best way to manage pain is to understand why that person or experience caused you pain. Once you are able to recognize the source of the pain in your life, you will be able to find ways to experience healing. God is the healer of all pain, and He shows us this through the passion, death, and resurrection of Jesus Christ. The pain that Jesus endured on Good Friday is not the end of Jesus' story—it is the beginning. Once Jesus handed over all the pain to the Father and said "Into your life I commend my Spirit," God removed his physical pain, and Jesus was able to complete his mission. We must have hope and believe that God will do the same for us in our own lives.

The dating fast is a period for you to focus on the areas of your life where there is pain and identify ways in which you can experience healing. Bring all of your pain to God and hand it over to Him. Ask Him to heal you, and He will. Open your heart to Him, and He will show you how you can experience healing.

As you begin to heal, you may realize that even when the intensity of the pain subsides, residual pain still exists within your heart. Some experiences may be so traumatic that they have completely changed your life, and the pain experienced will never be fully removed. There should be comfort, however, knowing what caused you pain and believing that God will eventually explain why you had to feel that pain—even if it is only when you meet Him in heaven. Continue to pray, and ask Him to heal your heart. Believe in Him, and He will help you persevere through the pain so it does not control your life.

Remember that even though you may heal from the pain in your past during this fast, this does not mean you'll be protected from future pain. Pain is an inevitable part of our humanity; however, the graces and understanding you receive from learning how to manage pain should help you protect your heart in the future and understand how to deal with painful experiences. Know that God is with you always and is the Healer of all pain.

The worst thing you can do with your pain is to deny that it exists. To overcome pain, start by acknowledging that you have it. This can be difficult, but it is the only way to move forward.

DARE: Make a list of all the people in your life who have caused you pain. Why did this person or experience cause you pain? What did they do that was so painful? Spend time thinking about these questions in prayer. When you are done, burn the list using the flame from a candle. Be sure to do this in a safe place away from other flammable items. As the paper begins to disintegrate, watch the candle (which may be thought of as the Light of Christ) consume the paper. Christ's love can disintegrate all pain, no matter how deep.

Forgiving others

Luke 6:27–31: "But to you who hear I say, love your enemies, do good to those who hate you, bless those who curse you, pray for those who mistreat you. To the person who strikes you on one cheek, offer the other one as well, and from the person who takes your cloak, do not withhold even your tunic. Give to everyone who asks of you, and from the one who takes what is yours do not demand it back. Do to others as you would have them do to you."

Forgiveness is always a difficult thing to do, but especially with someone who hurts you. It can take people many months, years, and even an entire lifetime to forgive others. Pride, pain, anger, frustration, and hurt usually stand in the way. Many people believe that when you forgive someone, you are accepting their actions and ignoring the reality of the situation. This could not be more false. By forgiving someone, you are not praising their actions or neglecting the pain they inflicted upon you, but rather you are acknowledging their actions, understanding the pain that it caused, and pushing your heart to see past the pain in order to open your heart to love again.

Forgiveness is more than just a word: it is a change of heart that leads to action. As Luke 6:27–31 states, we must love, do good, extend blessings, and pray for our enemies.

Forgiveness involves both words and actions, and these actions must originate from a change of heart. When this change occurs, you may experience peace within your heart. This peace occurs because you have freed your heart to love again. When you fail to forgive others, however, you are not only hurting the other person—you are also hurting yourself. The vengeance, hatred, anger, frustration, and pain that you build within your heart are an enormous burden to carry, negatively affecting you and all your other relationships. The only way to free yourself from this burden is to truly have a change of heart and forgive those who cause you pain. Are you struggling to forgive others? Then use the time of this dating fast to ask God to help you have a change of heart and forgive. Read the Bible, and look to Jesus as a perfect example for how we are called to forgive.

It has rightly been said that holding a grudge does nothing to hurt the other person—the only person it continues to hurt is yourself. Stop binding yourself to the chains of pain. You do not need to forget, but you must forgive.

DARE: Think again about the person who has hurt you, and offer a rosary for them. Continue to pray for them beyond today.

Forgiving yourself and accepting God's forgiveness

Proverbs 28:13; Ephesians 4:32 "People who cover over their sins will not prosper. But if they confess and forsake them, they will receive mercy"; "Be kind to one another, compassionate, forgiving one another as God has forgiven you."

There are many elements of forgiveness. In addition to forgiving others, you must learn how to forgive yourself. This concept can be difficult to comprehend. Without realizing it, you may well be your own harshest critic. This is not what God wants for you. God wants you to be happy in this life. He understands that you are human and fallible. Like everyone, you will make mistakes that hurt others and yourself. Do not beat yourself up for things that happened in your past. Once you show remorse for your sins and ask for God's forgiveness, you are forgiven, and you must believe that you are forgiven.

If God your almighty Father and Creator has forgiven you, why not dare to forgive yourself?

Reflect on this question and think about what obstacles stand in the way of accepting your own forgiveness. If you are struggling with this, ask God for His help. Ask Him to touch your heart in a special way to show you that He has forgiven you and that you can and should forgive yourself.

Throughout the dating fast, keep your mind and heart open to allow God to show you that you are once again forgiven and free to love. Always remember that perfectionism is not the same thing as holiness. God loves us for who we are, what we have done, and who we will become. He loves us regardless of what we do or do not do. God's love is infinite.

Pray the prayer below before you go to bed tonight. Continue to pray this prayer in the evenings if forgiveness is something that you especially need to receive during this fast.

> Jesus, through the power of the Holy Spirit, go back to my memory as I sleep. Every hurt that has been done to me—heal that hurt. Every hurt that I have caused to another person—heal that hurt. All the relationships that are damaged that I am not aware of—heal those relationships. But, Lord, if there is anything I need to do, if I need to go to a person because he is still suffering from my hand, bring to me awareness of that person. I choose to forgive and ask to be forgiven. Remove whatever bitterness may be in my heart, Lord, and fill the empty spaces with your love. Thank you, Jesus. I love you. Amen.

DARE: Pray the prayer above and write a letter to everyone you owe an apology to, including yourself and God. What would you tell these people if you could?

Understanding mercy

Wisdom 15:1–2 "But you, our God, are good and true, slow to anger, and governing all with mercy. For even if we sin, we are yours, and know your might; but we will not sin, knowing that we belong to you."

God is a *merciful Father*. This may be a phrase that you have heard before since it is used within the Church. Even though it is frequently spoken, however, I have realized that many people are unable to explain how God is a merciful Father – in fact, they cannot define mercy.

Mercy is "the act of sparing or the forbearance of a violent act expected" (*Webster's*). Using this definition, God's mercy is evident when He spares us from judgment and harm. Through Jesus Christ we are granted mercy for all eternity. It is His pure and precious blood that cleanses us from all sin. This is an inalienable right we are given by God. He will grant us mercy even if we do not ask for it. Yet, it is through the act of asking that we are able to recognize our need for His mercy. As the Bible passage from the book of Wisdom says, "For even if we sin, we are yours, and know your might." This passage emphasizes that God extends His mercy upon us regardless of our present state in life. Even when we sin, God's mercy for us continues to reign.

St. Maria Faustina is known for revealing the chaplet of divine mercy to the world. During her lifetime she received visions from Christ urging her to create an image depicting God's mercy for all humanity. She obeyed his command and created a beautiful image of Christ that reveals His Most Sacred Heart and illustrates His mercy. If you do not own a copy of it, you can find it on the Internet; a copy of the prayers is also included in today's dare. Within the painting, the pale ray stands for the Water that makes souls righteous; the red ray stands for the Blood that is the life of souls. At the bottom of the painting are written the words "Jesus, I trust in you." In addition to the painting, there is also a chaplet we can say to contemplate God's mercy for us and ask Him to continue to extend His mercy upon the whole world.

DARE: Say a Divine Mercy chaplet using rosary beads. As you pray, contemplate God's mercy for you.

On rosary beads, "First say one 'Our Father,' 'Hail Mary,' and 'The Creed.'

Then on the Our Father beads, say: 'Eternal Father, I offer You the Body and Blood, Soul and Divinity of Your dearly beloved Son, Our Lord Jesus Christ, in atonement for our sins and those of the whole world.'

On the Hail Mary beads, say: 'For the sake of His sorrowful Passion have mercy on us and on the whole world.'

In conclusion, say three times: 'Holy God, Holy Mighty One, Holy Immortal One, have mercy on us and on the whole world.'

Conclude with the following prayer: 'Eternal Father, in whom mercy is endless and the treasury of compassion inexhaustible. Look kindly upon us and increase your mercy in us, so that in difficult moments we might not despair nor become despondent, but with great confidence submit ourselves to your Holy will, which is love and mercy itself. O Blood and Water, which gushed forth from the Heart of Jesus as a fount of mercy for us, I trust in You.'"

16

Believing in God's compassion

Psalm 86:15: "But you, O Lord, are a compassionate and gracious God, slow to anger, abounding in love and faithfulness."

Compassion is profound sympathy for the suffering of another person. Without compassion, we cannot truly care for someone else – it instills a desire to help the person in need. God not only cares about us but is compassionate towards us, and He used Jesus as an example to show us His compassion. Knowing about and believing in this aspect of God should create a kind of peace within your heart. God has a compassionate heart for you, and it began before you were born, before you ever lived on this earth and knew that you would need compassionate people in your life. Jeremiah 1:5 states, "Before I formed you in the womb I knew you, before you were born I set you apart."

Consider how Jesus testified to compassion. During His life, He extended God's compassion to all people, including women. One of the most recognized stories of Jesus' compassion with women is recorded in John 8:1–11: *"Then each went to his house, while Jesus went to the Mount of Olives. But early in the morning he arrived again in the temple area, and all the people started coming to him, and he sat down and taught them. Then the scribes and the Pharisees brought a*

He is patient with us + our transgressions.

woman who had been caught in adultery and made her stand in the middle. They said to him, 'Teacher, this woman was caught in the very act of committing adultery. Now in the law, Moses commanded us to stone such women. So what do you say?' They said this to test him, so that they could have some charge to bring against him. Jesus bent down and began to write on the ground with his finger. But when they continued asking him, he straightened up and said to them. 'Let the one among you who is without sin be the first to throw a stone at her.' Again he bent down and wrote on the ground. And in response, they went away one by one, beginning with the elders. So he was left alone with the woman before him. Then Jesus straightened up and said to her, 'Woman, where are they? Has no one condemned you?' She replied, 'No one, sir.' Then Jesus said, 'neither do I condemn you. Go and from now on do not sin any more.'

What compassion Christ showed! While recognizing that her behavior was sinful, he did not judge her for her wrongdoing, but extended His compassion upon her and challenged other people to do the same. Believe in God's compassionate Truth and let it permeate your heart throughout your dating fast.

DARE: Reflect on the gospel passage above and imagine yourself as the woman in this story. What is Jesus revealing to you in this passage about His compassion for you?

Why didn't we write 'put' instead of saying it?

How relieved the woman must have felt

We are forgiven no matter what, even by a God who is without sin, unlike us....

Good Friday and Easter
(Death and the Cross)

Luke 23:42–43; Jude 2 "Then he said, 'Jesus, remember me when you come into your kingdom.' He replied to him, 'Amen I say to you, today you will be with me in Paradise.'" "May mercy, peace, and love be yours in abundance."

I once heard someone say that the most beautiful thing on earth is the cross. This idea can be confusing to people, especially if they are not Christian. After all, crucifixion is a horrible and torturous way for anyone to die, let alone our Savior. But as Christians we are taught to look beyond the crucifixion. The cross does not only signify Good Friday—it also illustrates the joy, hope, and love of Easter Sunday, the Resurrection of our Lord.

The cross is a symbol of strength. On the cross, Jesus absorbs the violence of the world, fights sins by taking them away, and becomes One with the Father. The lance that pierced Christ's side, causing blood and water to flow out, has both an external and internal meaning about the capacity of Christ's love for us. The external sign is reflected by the physical penetration into the heart and side of Christ, while the internal sign is God's love and mercy that was poured out of Christ for us.

The cross is a symbol for joy and peace. Jesus' love for each of us is shown on the cross, and it is God's love that brings the peace that the world cannot give. It is this joy and peace that makes our hearts pure just as the Resurrection freed our hearts to be pure for all eternity. Just as Jesus endured the pain of the cross in order to unite Him to the Father, so too, we may also experience our own crosses to align us closer to Our Father. Some crosses may be life's major disasters, while others are everyday discomforts and distresses. Regardless of the weight of each cross in our lives, they all have the same purpose: to test our faith, trust, and hope in God in order to bring us closer to the resurrection.

As Christians we believe that every Good Friday is followed by an Easter Sunday. For every death there is new life in Christ. God allowed His only Son to die on the cross for our sins so that we may live eternally with Him. Jesus freely chose to die for our sins. He thought about us as He was hanging on the cross and continued to pray for us until He passed away. When He died He descended into Hell and then rose on the third day to spend eternity with the Father in Heaven. He opened the gates of Heaven so that we might have eternal life. He loved us so much that He endured all of that pain and suffering for our benefit. While God does not owe us anything, He freely gives us everything because He loves us that much. The cross is now a symbol of His infinite love for us.

DARE: Sit in a church or chapel and stare at a crucifix. Reflect on the passion and crucifixion of the Lord. Imagine him telling you, "I did all of this for you—just you." How does this make you feel? Are you able to accept that it is true? Write a letter to God about your experience.

The Sacrament of Reconciliation

Hebrews 10:22 "Let us go right into the presence of God, with true hearts fully trusting him. For our evil consciences have been sprinkled with Christ's blood to make us clean, and our bodies have been washed with pure water."

While Jesus was on earth He institutionalized the sacraments as a means for us to uniquely experience God's presence. Each of the sacraments grants the person receiving them special graces. The sacrament of reconciliation focuses on forgiveness and peace. During this sacrament, you reflect on your previous sins and humbly come before the priest to confess what is on your heart. Your heart may be heavy due to fighting with a friend or family member. Maybe you told a lie or were manipulative in a business dealing. Whatever the sin may be, ask God to give you the grace to come to Him with a contrite and humble heart. As Catholics we believe that God speaks through the priest and blesses us with His compassion and mercy.

Many people take the graces of this sacrament for granted and only go to confession when they feel it is absolutely necessary. (Or, worse, even then they do not go.) It is important to remember that God allows us to celebrate the sacrament of reconciliation as often as we want, even daily. The more we attend reconciliation, the more He will grace our lives with His peace, forgiveness, and love. So during the dating fast, why not resolve to attend this sacrament at least once a month? I guarantee that it will start to transform your life and fill you with a greater awareness of God's presence and mercy. In addition, since all of the sacraments are intertwined, the more you frequent the sacrament of confession and are given the grace of a clean heart, the more pure you will be when you receive the body and blood of Christ during the sacrament of the Eucharist at mass.

Like all sacraments, the sacrament of reconciliation helps you to become more virtuous. Reconciliation helps you to honestly reflect on the areas of your life where you have fallen short. Reconciliation enables you to exercise strength to confess your sins and humbly come before God and the priest in the confessional. After you state your sins, God extends His mercy and offers you peace. It is incredible to think that God loves us so much that He gives us a sacrament to show us His mercy and help us to become more in union with Him.

DARE: Go to confession. Take the letter you wrote on Day 17 with you, and use that as the meditation before going in to speak with the priest.

Receiving peace

John 16:33 "I have told you this so that you might have peace in me. In the world you will have trouble, but take courage, I have conquered the world."

Jesus is the Prince of Peace. Jesus said "My peace I leave with you, my peace I give to you." So in order to understand Christ and His presence in your life, it is important to recognize and obtain peace. We are all capable of receiving the grace of peace as long as we are open to Christ. If we humbly ask for His peace, patiently wait, and open our mind and heart to the inner workings of the Holy Spirit, we will be granted peace.

Padre Pio said that "peace is order, it is the harmony in each one of us, it is a continual joy that is born in witnessing a clear conscience; it is the holy joy of a heart wherein God reigns." Since love only resides in peace and God *is* love, only He can provide us with the peace we desire. So it is important to seek God in order to obtain peace within our own lives and be graced with love.

It is easy to talk about the value of peace, but you may wonder how you can obtain it. St. Francis de Sales outlines three ways: "let us have the very pure intention of will to do all things for the honor and glory of God; let us do the little that we can toward that end, according to the advice of our spiritual director; and let us leave it to God to take care of all the rest." As this saint shows us, peace comes from purity of heart. It comes from surrounding ourselves with influential people of faith and surrendering ourselves to God so that we may come to completely trust in His ways. Peace is greater than a feeling of happiness; it is certitude of mind and heart that creates a stillness and calmness within the depths of your soul.

DARE: Spend time doing something that gives you peace. If possible, share this experience with a friend. Reflect on this experience. What aspects of it allowed you to receive peace?

Thanksgiving

2 Thessalonians 1:3 "We ought to thank God always for you, brothers, as is fitting, because your faith flourishes ever more, and the love of every one of you for one another grows even greater."

Many parents teach their children to say "please" and "thank you" when asking for or receiving things from others. These remarks are seen as a sign of respect and gratitude for the person's gifts or kind gestures. As individuals grow up, they often forget to say "please" or "thank you." Without having the constant reminder from a parent or guardian, these phrases begin to drop out of their vocabulary. People assume that the other person already knows about their appreciation.

This loss of explicit gratitude is unfortunate. Words of gratitude are not only used to show respect, but also to create humility. Reflecting on all the things you are thankful for, and then expressing that thanks, can help you realize just how fortunate you are. We all have many things to be thankful for, the most significant one being the gift of life. God loved us so much that He brought us to existence in order to give us the opportunity to live freely and choose to love Him back. This is such an amazing gift! There are many other gifts we can be thankful for as well: family, friends, relationships, food, water, shelter, clothing, or life experiences and opportunities.

Even the secular American world recognizes the importance of gratitude by celebrating a day of thanks every year in November. Thanksgiving is my favorite holiday. You may ask why. Why would this be my favorite holiday, especially above all the other wonderful and joyous holidays throughout the year? My answer is this: Thanksgiving is about sharing a meal together with those whom you love. As you read earlier, cooking is one of my favorite things to do, and Thanksgiving allows me to carry out this passion in full force as I help my mother prepare the Thanksgiving feast.

Furthermore, Thanksgiving is about simplicity. It invites you to focus on the people you are with—family or friends—and be present with them. It is about fostering those relationships and spending time with people you may not see very often. Finally, of course, Thanksgiving is about giving thanks for the many blessings you were given the previous year. One of my favorite family traditions is going around the kitchen table at Thanksgiving and sharing what we are thankful for and why. We also share one aspect or quality from each family member and why we are thankful for their presence in our lives. This experience has brought my family closer together.

You can do something similar every day. Thanksgiving should not be the only day when you offer thanks to God and others. During the dating fast and continuing afterwards, make it a habit to end your day with a simple prayer of thanks for everything that you have been given, but most importantly for the gift of life and for God's love.

DARE: Create a list of everything you are thankful for. Post the list in a place you frequently visit or see. Do not just write what the thing is but also why you are thankful for it.

Finding the strength within

Proverbs 31:25; 2 Corinthians 12:10 "She is clothed with strength and dignity, and she laughs at the days to come." "When I am weak, then I am strong."

All women are graced with the gift of strength. After all, God chose us to be the child bearers and play a crucial role in the plan of salvation. He recognized the strength of women and continues to acknowledge this today. Throughout the Bible, Christ has revealed the strength of women, but just like with the women in the Bible, it will take time for God to reveal to you your own strength. The best way to identify your strength is to reflect on your past and recognize the tough experiences God helped you overcome. In what weak moments of your life did He strengthen you? As Mother Teresa says, "You are not strong because of the great things you do, but because of the small things you do with great love." By turning to God and reaching out to Him in faith, you will always be strong.

One of the richest moments when I was graced with strength occurred during one of my weakest moments. At the time I was struggling with great inner pain and suffering. I didn't love myself and felt completely unworthy of love. I had a lot of broken relationships in my life, some that I caused and others that were the result of other people's actions. I felt so weak and helpless that I began to question

Christ's presence in my life. During one winter break, I decided to go on a service retreat to West Virginia to build and repair houses. One afternoon, I was standing outside with my team in order to build a deck for a couple that had very few material things. I was shocked to witness a degree of poverty I had never seen before. The temperature that day was in the single digits, and no matter how much I moved around I was freezing cold. At the end of the afternoon, I looked at the completed deck, and tears began to roll down my face. For the first time in a long time, I felt strong. Despite my own inner feelings of weakness, I had helped build a deck (something I hadn't known how to do 6 hours earlier) and helped someone who was less fortunate.

Strength is not a one-time gift that you receive. Christ continues to give you strength daily. His omnipotent presence is always with you, even when you do not see or feel Him. As you begin the second half of your dating fast, be mindful of how He works in your own life to help you conquer the world. How does Christ continue to give you strength? Celebrate those moments when they occur, and remember those moments later, especially during difficult times. These experiences will remind you that you are a strong woman of God.

DARE: So that you can be stronger in the worst of situations, try an experiment during the situations that aren't so bad. Smile all day and do not complain about anything. Maintain that smile throughout the day, no matter how many distractions and difficulties you face. At the end of the day write about your experiences, and challenge yourself to continue to do this every day, especially in the moments that require extra strength.

22

Learning how to be alone

Psalm 1:1–3 "Happy those who do not follow the counsel of the wicked, nor go the way of sinners, nor sit in company with scoffers. Rather, the law of the Lord is their joy; God's law they study day and night. They are like a tree planted near streams of water, that yields its fruit in season; its leaves never wither; whatever they do prospers."

Recently some of my friends completed an online questionnaire about themselves. One of the questions asked about people's greatest fear. The greatest fear expressed was *being alone*. This is not surprising. As social human beings, it makes sense that we want to feel connected. We do not want to feel lonely, especially since we are created to be social. Yet most people are not aware of the difference between being alone and loneliness. A person can be surrounded by people and still feel lonely. Conversely, a person can be alone and not feel lonely. *Alone* is a state of being you may not have control over. Depending on your present state in life, there may be times that require you to be alone. You may live alone or have moved to a new city where you don't know many people yet. You might be tempted to fill the emptiness with things and stuff. You might spend hours a day watching TV, preoccupy yourself with relationships that are not healthy for you or the other person, or spend time being lazy and complaining about being bored.

But you don't ever have to feel lonely or to flee the feeling of loneliness. God is always with you, even when you do not see or feel His presence. As you continue on the dating fast alone (not in a relationship), my hope is that you will begin to embrace the alone time that you have rather than fearing it. Learn to enjoy the moments of peace and quiet when it is just God and you. You have the choice: to feel lonely while you are alone, or to accept the alone time that you have with God and let it fill you with a peace and joy that no human could ever offer. Learn to bask in the presence of God, and you will never feel lonely again because you will know that He is always by your side.

Every person should learn how to be alone. There is a peace that comes from being alone and accepting the present state of your life. This does not mean that God is calling you to a permanent life of solitude. All God wants is some time to show you how much you are loved and how to best serve Him on this earth so that you can spend eternity with Him. Give Him time now, and He will reward you for eternity. Listen to the inner workings of your heart, and you will learn how to listen to others. Be still, and you will learn how to support others. Free yourself from all of the things in your life that enslave you, and you will be open to giving and receiving love. The best way to learn these truths is to spend alone time with God. During these times you will begin to recognize that the majority of people you encounter who are surrounded by other people are still lonely. What makes the difference is your awareness of God's presence in your life.

DARE: Think about the time in your life that you were most aware of God's presence in your daily life. Recall the peace and happiness you felt. What was it about this experience that brought you joy?

23

Finding companions on the journey

1 Corinthians 12:12–27 "The body is a unit, though it is made up of many parts; and though all its parts are many, they form one body. So it is with Christ. For we were all baptized by one Spirit into one body—whether Jews or Greeks, slave or free—and we were all given the one Spirit to drink. Now the body is not made up of one part but of many. If the foot should say, 'Because I am not a hand, I do not belong to the body,' it would not for that reason cease to be part of the body. And if the ear should say, 'Because I am not an eye, I do not belong to the body,' it would not for that reason cease to be part of the body. If the whole body were an eye, where would the sense of hearing be? If the whole body were an ear, where would the sense of smell be? But in fact God has arranged the parts in the body, every one of them, just as he wanted them to be. If they were all one part, where would the body be? As it is, there are many parts, but one body. The eye cannot say to the hand, 'I don't need you!' And the head cannot say to the feet, 'I don't need you!' On the contrary, those parts of the body that seem to be weaker are indispensable, and the parts that we think are less honorable we treat with special honor. And the parts that are unpresentable are treated with special modesty, while our presentable parts need no special treatment. But God has combined the members of the body and has given greater honor to the parts that lacked it, so that there should be no division in the body, but that its parts should have equal concern for each other. If one part suffers, every part suffers with it; if one part is honored, every part rejoices with it. Now you are the body of Christ, and each one of you is a part of it."

What a transformation it would be if all of us saw ourselves as members of the same body of Christ! As the popular hymn "Companions on the Journey" suggests, we are partners on a journey to get to Heaven, and we are called to live in communion with one another. We all have something unique to offer that no one else can fully provide. We are all brothers and sisters in Christ who are sons and daughters of Our Heavenly Father. Each part of the body of Christ is necessary and vital to the makeup and function of the whole body—the Church. God has united us on this earth in order to support, challenge, and bring each other closer to Him. God understands our fallen human nature and the need to have companions on the journey who will provide support, guidance, wisdom, happiness, and joy along the way. God recognized humanity's need for community already with the first human. When He created Adam, He knew that Adam could not be alone, so He created Eve to be with him. God knows that we should not be alone, and he will provide you with people to make your life more joyful, peaceful, and beautiful. Remain open to the people that God is placing in your life.

DARE: Think about the companions you have had in your life. Who would you consider a companion? Why? What qualities did they bring to your life? Did they embody attributes that you also hope to attain? Write one of them a letter that thanks them for being a companion on your journey.

24

How friendship leads
to self-discovery

Sirach 6:14 "A faithful friend is a sturdy shelter; he who finds one finds a treasure. A faithful friend is beyond price, no sum can balance its worth."

Friendship is an important concept to understand on the dating fast. You might think that since you are on a fast, you must isolate yourself from others and focus on yourself. Yet although you are concentrating on yourself and your relationship with God, you must not forget to maintain those relationships close to your heart—friends and family. These people will be able to show you things that you could never discover on your own.

We've heard it said that if you want to know more about someone, spend time with her family and friends. It's true for ourselves as well—the people we surround ourselves with have a tremendous influence on who we become. Therefore, it is vital for you to surround yourself with positive and influential people of Christ who will propel you closer to God. If you choose to enrich your life with these people of character, you will be forever changed in a positive way. Find people who will lead you to Christ and inspire you to achieve greatness. Bask in the beauty of these relationships, and feed off of one another in order to propel each other closer to God.

When I started my dating fast, I spent the first two weeks in solitude and quiet prayer. I maintained a very strict regimen and isolated myself from other people because I thought that was what God wanted. Two weeks later, God placed a guy friend in my life to help me discover some very important lessons. This friend showed me so much about myself. We cooked together, rode bikes together, swam together, had long discussions, and taught each other the essence of genuine friendship. Without him, I do not believe I would have gained as much insight and personal awareness as I did on my fast. He taught me that I loved to cook and share meals with a small group of people. He fostered my passion for being outdoors and my love of exercise. So much of myself that was lost or neglected in previous dating relationships was restored through this friendship. He showed me that people do care about my heart and can spend time getting to know me without letting the physical aspect get in the way. He also showed me that I needed to be with someone who not only allows me to practice my faith, but also shares my beliefs and would be a prayer warrior for me.

I am eternally grateful for this person and for the lesson I learned about the importance of friendship. Therefore, I cannot emphasize enough the importance of allowing friendships to grow within your life while you are on this fast. While you refrain from dating or pursuing anyone romantically, you will have the opportunity to focus on people's hearts and discover a new part of your own heart in the process.

DARE: Your friendships teach you how to let in complete strangers and love them to the best of your abilities. Call a friend you haven't talked to in a while and have a good conversation with them.

25

Understanding sexual attraction and sexual embrace

1 Thessalonians 1:4 "God loves you, you have been chosen."

During your fast, you must reflect on the purpose of sexual attraction so you can properly and purposefully practice that in future relationships. Sexual attraction is something that you feel toward another person, and it heightens your interest in them. It is meant to lead you to want to discover more about the other person. Sexual attraction is an important part of relationships; however, it is not the most important part and should not be the foundation of a relationship. Sexual attraction only becomes a problem when you carry out impure actions because of it. In order to have meaningful dating relationships, it is important to understand what the Church's teachings are on sex and marriage and why they exist. The explanation behind these teachings will further your understanding of genuine love and relationships.

The Church views sex as a marital embrace between man and woman. Both men's and women's bodies are holy temples that house the Holy Spirit, and thus each person must respect the other person's body as well as their own. By restraining from unchaste actions in a dating relationship, you are giving a beautiful gift to the Lord through your obedience. You are also exhibiting true charity through the gift of responsibility and respect. You show these virtues to the other person and to yourself. All women are called to be respectful in order to build up "godly men." This is a profound grace that God grants to all women.

Within a dating relationship, chastity allows you to see beyond the lust for and physical attraction of the person and truly appreciate the individual. Chastity is a choice all humans are capable of making and practicing. Regardless of your sexual past, you must focus on your current chastity convictions and live your life accordingly. Chastity does not ignore the beauty of the person but unveils the true identity of who they are. Through a dating fast you can practice chastity and grow in self-respect and charity of God and others. You will be prepared to find the man who will put your soul above his own physical pleasures. This type of person could be the one God is calling you to date and discern the vocation of marriage with.

Being married is a bond that unites a man and woman where they recommit their lives to one another and physically express the vows they took on their wedding day, through the act of sex. Sex in marriage is an act of love that is free, total, faithful, and fruitful. In contrast, all sex acted outside of marriage says "I love you, but..." Sex outside of marriage uses people as a means to an end in order to receive physical pleasure or experience a false sense of intimacy. This love is solely based on feelings and is not free and total. True love should express that you "will the other person heaven."

True love involves dying to yourself for the greater good of the other person. In a dating relationship, this type of love is acted through obedience, self-control, respect, and responsibility for the other person and their body. If a couple does not make any physical sacrifices during dating, there will be no foundation for sacrifices when they enter into marriage. A celibate dating relationship allows both people to test their abilities to exercise self-control and still be faithful to one another in the relationship. This is an excellent indicator of what their faithfulness and commitment will be in their future marriage. It is only when you totally give of yourself to the other person on the altar during the marriage ceremony that you are able to truthfully engage in sex as an act arising from love and for the sake of love.

DARE: Too often, women rely on sex as a way of feeling affirmed that they are beautiful. As one way of growing closer to Christ, discover the beauty within yourself. Spend 10 minutes today in prayer asking God to show you your inner beauty. To God, there is no one in the world more beautiful than you. Become aware of how God chooses to reveal your beauty, including through peacefulness that touches your heart after your prayer.

26

Purity

Matthew 5:8 "Blessed are the pure in heart, for they will see God."

Though it is a great virtue, purity is seldom praised in our culture. Society undermines purity by propagating lies to young women that we are prudes to even think about purity, let alone exercise or practice it in our lives. And if you fail at practicing purity, for whatever reason, society tells you that you will never be pure again.

But purity is much more than whether or not you refrain from having sex until marriage. Yes, it is important to save yourself for your future spouse. But purity refers to what is on your heart, your intentions. The Beatitudes teach us "Blessed are the pure in heart for they shall see God." Even after you get married and have sex with your spouse, you will still need to uphold your purity of heart, as well as the purity of your spouse and children. It is purity that will allow you to see God and to show others the path to Him.

Purity is a grace that God gives each person when they are born. God's hope for His children is that they will maintain a pure heart in order to maintain an intimate relationship with Him. A pure heart is an honest and true heart that is open to the love of God. A pure heart is reflective and meditative, spending moments of silence throughout the dating fast to ponder the Holy Spirit's inner workings and movements. It is a heart that works in conjunction with the mind to understand and know how to live a life of faith and charity.

DARE: Look at yourself in the mirror for 10 minutes and tell yourself that you are beautiful. Try to imagine the beauty and purity that God sees when He looks at you. Do not focus on any flaws or imperfections, because that is not what God sees. Remind yourself throughout this exercise that you are a beautiful daughter of God. You are His chosen daughter.

Serving others before yourself

Matthew 25:34–40 "Then the king will say to those on his right, 'Come you who are blessed by my Father. Inherit the kingdom prepared for you from the foundation of the world. For I was hungry and you gave me food, I was thirsty and you gave me drink, a stranger and you welcomed me, naked and you clothed me, ill and you cared for me, in prison and you visited me.' Then the righteous will answer him and say, 'Lord, when did we see you hungry and feed you, or thirsty and give you drink? When did we see you a stranger and welcome you, or naked and clothe you? When did we see you ill or in prison and visit you?' And the king will say to them in reply, 'Amen, I say to you, whatever you did for one of these least brothers of mind, you did for me.'"

We are social creatures called to live in union with one another. As people of faith, we recognize the many gifts God bestows in our lives. Regardless of the obstacles and trials we may face, we are able to see the beauty of God in everything and everyone. God calls us to live in this world and be an example of Christ to all whom we encounter daily. This is a high standard that Our Father challenges each of us to meet. There are people in the world who are suffering, and we should be a source of inspiration and hope for the people who are unable to see the beauty of the cross, who do not know that for every death there is new life. For many people, you may be the closest encounter they have with God!

Even people who are not spiritually suffering may need assistance with more basic daily needs: shelter, food, finances, or clothing. We must learn how to be compassionate towards strangers and look at every person with the eyes of Christ. We must recognize the God-given dignity of each person and provide love and support where it is needed. On this 27th day of your dating fast, ask yourself how you can help others around you. What gifts do you have that can be shared with others?

Sometimes we are tempted to give our money or time only when we have the extra means. But God demands us to help others not only from our surplus, but also from our primary allotment. We must trust in God and offer a portion of ourselves as a small sacrifice to extend our offering, even when it may be a challenge. It is only when we give ourselves completely that we are truly giving anything at all. Though we should be prudent with what we are capable of offering, we need to honestly reflect on what we can give and make that sincere offer of ourselves rather than merely giving only what is convenient. Recognize the areas of your life that demand a small sacrifice in order to truly serve others. Remember that when you serve others, you serve Christ.

DARE: Today, complete one random act of kindness or perform one act of service for another individual. What activity did you choose? What did you learn about yourself from this experience?

Commitment

1 Thessalonians 3:11–13 "Now may God himself, our Father, and our Lord Jesus direct our way to you, and may the Lord make you increase and abound in love for one another and for all, just as we have for you, so as to strengthen your hearts, to be blameless in holiness before our God and Father at the coming of our Lord Jesus with all his holy ones."

Love is a commitment and promise. It is a genuine choice to be vulnerable with another person for the rest of your life. This type of commitment is based on a profound choice and not fleeting emotions or feelings. When you commit to love someone, you promise to love them for eternity. You choose that person for who they are, were, and will become. You promise to be faithful and true and persevere throughout all of life's joys and obstacles.

God commits Himself to us every day during every moment of our life. God does not need us to survive; yet He promises to love us regardless of whether we love Him back. God will love us through the good times and the bad, in sickness and in health, and for the rest of eternity. His love is constant and will never change. The best example of God's love for us comes from Jesus Christ. Jesus' life on earth was meant for one purpose—to illustrate the capacity of God's infinite love and mercy and to carry out His commitment to each of us individually for the rest of eternity.

As humans, we are called to emulate Christ and strive for the perfection that God made within each of us. We must commit ourselves to God, just as He commits Himself to us. The relationships in our lives serve as instruments for us to learn how to be more committed individuals. When you commit to someone, you stand by your words, and your actions serve as a way to express that commitment. Commitment demands a definitive answer. Are you going to commit... yes or no? Christ chose yes! What is your response?

DARE: As a way of strengthening your ability to commit, make a commitment to yourself to complete one item on your bucket list (your life's To Do list) before you complete the dating fast. Be sure to commit to something that is both reasonable and practical considering the short time allotted for its completion. Make sure that you set a concrete date, and outline how you plan to carry out this action.

How confidence leads to hope

Luke 11:9–10; Proverbs 16:3 "And I tell you, ask and you will receive; seek and you will find; knock and the door will be opened to you. For everyone who asks, receives; and the one who seeks, finds; and to the one who knocks, the door will be opened." "Entrust your works to the Lord, and your plans will succeed."

Confidence is an important characteristic all young women should strive to embody. Confidence does not mean arrogance, but rather a humble strong presence that is determined to succeed. You must learn to be a confident individual, especially if you struggle with appreciating your self-worth. Confidently place yourself before God and ask Him to fill your heart with His love. Luke 11: 9–10 states that if you come before God and ask Him, you shall receive—all you have to do is have the confidence to ask, and the humility to listen and accept what is being given. So have the confidence! Think of yourself as a queen – most are portrayed in movies and books as confident rulers. So be a queen to your King, your heavenly Father. Have confidence in God, and He will show you how to have confidence in yourself. This confidence will give you the hope to believe in His faithfulness.

As St. John of the Cross, the wise Spanish mystic, says, "We obtain from God as much as we hope for Him. God does not give according to our merits, but according to our hope." This hope enables you to find your security, identity, and dependence on God. You have a unique value and dignity that is independent of what you do. No one can take away your God-given right to eternal happiness. Only you can stand in the way and make your happiness in this life more difficult. God will love you the same, regardless of what you do. He wants what is best for you. Believe this to be true, accept God's love, and have confidence and hope in the Lord.

DARE: If you could do anything in the world and there were no limitations or obstacles, what would you do? Why? Journal about these questions, and open your journaling session with a prayer to God to open your heart to great confidence.

Learning to take pleasure from life

Isaiah 55:1–3; 8–9 "All you who are thirsty come to the water! You who have no money, come, receive grain and eat; Come, without paying and without cost, drink wine and milk! Why spend your money for what is not bread; your wages for what fails to satisfy? Heed me, and you shall eat well, you shall delight in rich fare. Come to me heedfully, listen, that you may have life ... For my thoughts are not your thoughts, nor are your ways my ways, says the Lord. As high as the heavens are above the earth, so high are my ways above your ways and my thoughts above your thoughts.

What do you enjoy doing? How do you spend your free time or downtime? Every day you are given a precious gift from God, and that is the gift of life. It is your choice to accept that gift and determine how you will use it. Some days may be more stressful and busy than others, but if you prioritize and organize your life, you should be able to find some downtime during the week when you can enjoy life and bask in the beautiful masterwork that God has created for your pleasure.

Since we are all unique individuals, our interests and passions vary. Some people may enjoy the arts and other people may enjoy nature, while others enjoy athletics or sports. Some people have a sweet tooth while others prefer salty foods. Regardless of where your interests lie, it is important, as you reach Day 30 of your dating fast, to let yourself occasionally enjoy these pleasures. After all, God is the One who fills you with excitement and happiness when you are enjoying your favorite things.

God wants each of us to be happy. He wants us to enjoy life and to keep a sense of humor about the highs and lows. There is a time and place for everything, and this includes the time to enjoy the things in this life that make you happy. God placed these things in your life to help you see Him in all aspects of life.

Obviously, you don't want to become too dependent on these things. Nothing should stand in the way of your relationship with God. So maintain prudence and exercise self-control when needed. But every now and then, enjoy that chocolate, join the soccer league, or paint that picture you've always wanted to paint. As you enjoy these daily pleasures, thank God for giving you these gifts. God's presence is everywhere, but especially in the people, places, and things that bring you energy and life! True happiness will come from doing what you are created to do. Discovering that mission starts with understanding your interests and the things that make your heart smile.

DARE: Treat yourself to one of your favorite things (food, drink, candy, hobby, or interest), and journal about why you like this thing. Then offer a short prayer to God, thanking Him for the gift of this pleasure in your life.

31

The importance of family

Isaiah 44:3 "I will pour out my spirit upon your offspring, and my blessing upon your descendants."

We are all born into a family. Some of us are fortunate to grow up in more positive and loving environments, while others of us may have struggled from being raised in a broken family. Regardless of your family background, however, your family offers you insight into how to start a family of your own and provide for them—even if your parents did not take the time to teach you the essentials. If, as you reflect on your own family, you become aware of brokenness, humbly give thanks to God for the wisdom of knowing what not to do, and ask for the grace to be a better provider for your future family. If you were fortunate to grow up in a supportive and loving environment, thank God for blessing you with this family and allowing you a good example to emulate when you begin your start your own family. Use whatever life God has given you as a source of wisdom and reflection.

As Catholics we are given the witness of a perfect family. Jesus, Mary, and Joseph, the Holy Family, are the perfect example of a loving family, and we must strive to emulate them. Pray to each of them and ask them to bless your future family and help you become the best wife for your husband and the best mother for your children. Although we are human and thus incapable of perfection, we are given the graces to fulfill our calling even with all our limitations – to be perfectly imperfect. Your future family will be perfectly imperfect if you pray together and help each other strive for holiness. This holiness will arise from understanding your need for Christ and humbly coming before Him with loving open arms, asking for His mercy and grace in times of joy and sadness. Family can be an anchor that provides stability and support throughout life. My hope is that, if it is your calling to become a wife and mother, you can foster a family life that provides you with greater joy and peace.

DARE: Reflect on your own family and the positive lessons they taught you about growth in holiness and love for Christ. Spend 15 minutes in prayer for your future family. If you want, journal about your thoughts and reflections.

32

How genuine friendship reveals God

A Friendship Prayer: Dear Lord, Thank you for a special gift, one that cannot be bought for any amount of money. Thank you for a gift wrapped in beauty that is wonderful in all seasons and times. Thank you for a gift that is always near in times of need and brings great joy. Thank you for the gift that sparkles with freshness every day. Thank you for my friend. May I never take this gift for granted. Amen.

Who is a genuine friend? Is it someone you spend time with? Is it someone whose presence you enjoy? Is it someone who makes you smile and laugh? Or is there something more about this person? John 15:15 shows us how Christ understands true friendship. The verse states, "No longer do I call you slaves, for the slave does not know what his master is doing; but I have called you friends, for all things that I have heard from My Father I have made known to you."

In order to understand genuine friendship, we must first become friends with Christ. It is only He who can show us how to be a genuine friend to others. He is the true example of friendship: He loves us unconditionally, He listens, He cares, He gives us hope and inspiration, He fills us with joy and excitement, He provides us with daily pleasures that make our heart smile, He challenges us to achieve greatness,

He heals us when we are sick, He supports us when we fall, He strengthens us when we are weak, He is always there for us, and He wishes us eternity.

Christ is the exemplary friend to us, and He sets the standard for the type of friend we should be for others. Our genuine friendships will have very little to do with feelings, laughter, and enjoyment and will focus on holiness and salvation. The mark of genuine friendship is for each person to be who God created her to be and to be accepted as that person. Genuine friendship involves freedom of choice, accountability, truth, and forgiveness. Of course, some of our connections to others will bring us pleasure and make us feel good, but genuine friendship goes deeper. This type of friendship takes risks, overlooks faults and failures, and loves unconditionally. It is something God provides in your life in order to help you live in community and help you get to heaven. Genuine friends are the most priceless gift you can receive on this earth; they are more precious than time, money, power, or material possessions. So make use of this remarkable blessing. Develop friendships with people who will mirror Christ's image for you and be His flesh. In addition, continue to strengthen your relationship with Christ and ask Him to help you be a genuine friend to others. You must learn to establish a genuine friendship with God and others first before you enter into a genuine friendship with your future spouse.

DARE: Write down one holy quality or attribute about each person that is close to you in your life. Think about these individuals' positive influence on your life and offer a prayer for each of them.

Growth vs. healing

1 Thessalonians 5:23–24 "May the God of peace himself make you perfectly holy and may you entirely, spirit, soul, and body, be preserved blameless for the coming of our Lord Jesus Christ. The one who calls you is faithful, and he will also accomplish it."

As you continue on the dating fast, you will begin to grow in a positive way and heal from any pain through God's love and mercy. It is important to understand that while growth and healing are intertwined, they are not the same process. You can heal without growing and you can grow without fully healing. So it is important to reflect on how, although related, they are distinct processes.

Growth stems from understanding who you once were compared to where you are now. As you reflect on the past, you will begin to experience change and growth. The dating fast will inevitably create growth in at least one area of your life. You may grow to become a more compassionate and understanding person; you may grow to discern your vocation in life; or you may grow into a more contemplative lifestyle. All of us are growing (in the sense of changing) every day—make sure that you are growing in a positive way. Remember that you have sole responsibility in how you choose to grow, and no one else can make this decision for you.

Healing is different. It is a process that demands understanding your past, recognizing the pain that lingers within your heart, and letting that pain transform into something life-giving. You must identify the pain and face it in order to heal. Like growth, healing is a process that takes time. Depending on your situation, it may take several years to fully heal from something in your past. No matter how long it takes, however, you will need to set aside time to heal while you grow; otherwise, your growth will eventually plateau and leave you with the lingering pain that you never fully addressed. Together, healing and growth can lead to greater fulfillment and peace in this life through Christ's love and mercy.

DARE: Go for a walk and think about the ways in which you have grown and healed on the dating fast. Are there any areas of your life that still need healing? If so, identify them and ask God to fill your heart with His healing love and mercy. Thank God for all the ways that you have grown on the fast.

Following your dreams

Proverbs 29:18, Philippians 4:8–9. "Where there is no vision, a people will perish"; "Finally, brothers, whatever is true, whatever is honorable, whatever is just, whatever is pure, whatever is lovely, whatever is gracious, if there is any excellence and if there is anything worthy of praise, think about these things. Keep on doing what you have learned and received and heard and seen in me. Then the God of peace will be with you."

Dreaming big — imagining a rich future for ourselves — is not just something we learn from motivational books. Scripture itself illustrates the importance of dreams. Proverbs 29:18 suggests it is a matter of survival: "Where there is no vision, people will perish." Philippians 4:8–9 reveals the qualities that dreams, like all good things, should have. Our dreams should be true, honorable, just, pure, lovely, and gracious, and should derive from His Excellence.

Even if you've stopped dreaming, it's easy to start again. Remember how spontaneously you did it as a child? The act of dreaming can help you discover what is on your heart, especially if you are honest and true with your thoughts and intentions. Our lives are merely reflections of the questions we ask. So during your dating fast, spend time dreaming, and ask the big questions. *What do you most desire?*

Then reflect on what is fueling your dreams and desires. Is it mere passion, or is there a deeper and richer motive? For instance, if your goal is to get married and have a family, you must think about why you have this desire. Is it merely to protect your image and fulfill the "American dream" that society propagates, or is it because you long to raise children to be soldiers for Christ and to share the intimacy of love with another human being?

Identifying and understanding the reasons behind your dreams is beneficial to setting goals that you can strive to obtain. It will also help reveal whether or not your dreams are in line with the will of God. God's will is for us to be happy and to carry out the vocation that will best lead to our sanctification. Any desire that is not in line with God's will cannot ultimately lead you to happiness, so set goals that stem from your dreams and the dreams He has for you. Further contemplation of these dreams will reveal whether they bring you peace and joy and lead you closer to God. Have faith, and dream big!

DARE: Generate a list of individual accomplishments you want to achieve before you die. Now, reflect on how they fit into the big picture of living a life of holiness and doing God's will. Spend time in prayer with God about these reflections.

35

Heaven

Matthew 18:1–4 "At that time the disciples approached Jesus and said, 'Who is the greatest in the kingdom of heaven?' He called a child over, placed it in their midst, and said, 'Amen, I say to you, unless you turn and become like children, you will not enter the kingdom of heaven. Whoever humbles himself like this child is the greatest in the kingdom of heaven. And whoever receives one child such as this in my name receives me.'"

What is heaven to you? As a little girl, I thought heaven was a place in the sky. When I would look up at the clouds, I would think about all of the people who were with God in heaven. Other children might think of heaven as a place where you get to do whatever you want, whenever you want. Heaven is also thought of as a place where you get to become an angel and fly. The daughter of a friend of mine told me that heaven is a happy place where you get to play all day.

You have surely heard similar stories and have your own vision of what heaven will be like. Regardless of your idea of heaven, though, the truth is that we will not know what it is until we die. Only then will we be at the gates of heaven hoping to spend eternity with God, our Father. Therefore, we must concern ourselves today not with the characteristics of heaven but with the path to getting there. Christ gives us clear suggestions. As Matthew 18 states, "Amen I say to you, unless you turn and become like children, you will not enter the kingdom of heaven." We must become like children who totally entrust everything to Our Heavenly Father. We must be innocent, humble, pure, contrite, trusting, and dependent on God. If you've ever spent time with a young child who has not yet been corrupted with the ways of the world, you will recognize this innocence and purity of heart. As you continue on this final week of the dating fast, focus on obtaining these virtues so that you can grow closer to God and be one step closer to heaven.

DARE: Play with a child. Admire their innocence and trust. Think about how you can become more child-like in your life.

The vocation of motherhood for all women

Luke 1:46–55 "And Mary said, 'my soul proclaims the greatness of the Lord; my spirit rejoices in God my savior. For he has looked upon his handmaid's lowliness; behold, from now on will all ages call me blessed. The Mighty One has done great things for me, and holy is his name. His mercy is from age to age to those who fear him. He has shown might with his arm, dispersed the arrogant of mind and heart. He has thrown down the rulers from their thrones but lifted up the lowly. The hungry he has filled with good things; the rich he has sent away empty. He has helped Israel his servant, remembering his mercy, according to his promise to our fathers, to Abraham and to his descendants forever.'"

A mother's role is to love and nurture her children. As women, we are called to be mothers and teach the world how to love. God gives women a special grace within their hearts in order to show others how to love. Therefore, our lives should focus on teaching others how to love Him so that they can best love themselves and others.

All women are called to the vocation of motherhood, whether biological or spiritual. Christ gives this blessing to all women, just as he bestows the vocation of fatherhood to all men. Even those who are hardest of heart and numb to all emotions have the special grace to be mothers and fathers, if they choose to accept and nurture this gift from God. As a woman, it is a matter of reflecting on this grace and thinking about what type of motherhood God is calling you to: a mother who, without children, influences the lives of all those she prays for, or a mother who bears children and raises them to be faith-filled individuals. Similarly, men are called to be fathers who tend to the flock of the Church, or fathers who raise children and bring their family closer to God. What capacity of love has God instilled in your heart? What type of motherhood are you called to live on this earth so that you can spend eternity with Him?

Marriage is a vocation, meaning that it is a call from God to live your life a certain way. This vocation is not for every single woman. Some women are called to the single or religious life. Proper discernment and prayer with God will help you discover how God wants you to best serve Him. There is a book called *Discerning the Will of God: A Guide to Christian Decision Making*, that offers Catholics a way to see what God is calling them to do – which job, whether to marry, and if to marry, whom. I encourage you to read this book to help you with all your future decisions, especially regarding your vocation.

DARE: Spend 15 minutes in silence praying to Mother Mary, who united in herself the role of spiritual and physical mother. Ask for her maternal love and grace to protect you throughout your life, but especially during this dating fast. Ask Mary to help you become more virtuous and to give you the understanding and courage to become more like her.

Your future self

John 15:7; Ephesians 3:16–19 "If you remain in me and my words remain in you, ask for whatever you want and it will be done for you." "That he may grant you in accord with the riches of his glory to be strengthened with power through his Spirit in the inner self, and that Christ may dwell in your hearts through faith; that you, rooted and grounded in love, may have strength to comprehend with all the holy ones what is the breadth and length and height and depth, and to know the love of Christ that surpasses knowledge, so that you may be filled with all the fullness of God."

Once you are able to understand who you are, you can focus on who you want to become. Your future self is comprised of your hopes, dreams, desires, and aspirations derived from your past and present self. So once you have a clearer sense of your internal present self, you will better understand your future self. This understanding is important in shaping the woman you will become. While you set goals and future aspirations, remain open to God's will for your life. God wants what is best for you, and that may include something you are not even consciously aware of today. Open yourself to God, and He will provide for you in ways that you could never imagine. He will surpass your wildest dreams. God loves you with infinite compassion, mercy, and charity and He desires you, His most precious daughter, to spend eternity with Him. His will for your life is the path that will lead you to Him. Listen to His ways and hear His voice. Spend your life on earth growing closer to God and fulfilling the plan that He has set out for you. You are the best and only person capable of fulfilling this plan completely.

DARE: Journal about what type of woman you want to become. If there are things about yourself or your past that you could change, how would you change them? If certain things are out of your control, how can you start to accept those parts of yourself, knowing that they are not limitations or failures that define you, but rather lessons on your journey? Set goals for how you plan to become the woman that you want to be.

38

God's has a spouse for you, so never settle

Proverbs 31:10–12; Sirach 7:25 "When one finds a worthy wife, her value is far beyond pearls. Her husband, entrusting his heart to her, has an unfailing prize. She brings him good, and not evil, all the days of her life...Giving your daughter in marriage ends a great task; but give her to a worthy man."

Women are precious daughters of God, and our hearts must always reside in Him. God desires us as his daughters to be in union with men who will love us as He loves us and help us raise His children. God gives women the ability to nurture life within them. It is a beautiful gift that should be shared with a worthy and notable man of God. As Proverbs 31:10–12 states, God values women so much that He says we are more valuable than pearls. If you want to know how God loves you, reflect on this Bible passage and know that you are precious, valuable, worthy, and loved. The type of man that God is calling you to marry will also understand the wisdom reflected in this passage and have the same thoughts and feelings for you. Such a man will want to honor and love you all the days of your life; in the good times and the bad, in sickness and in health, until death. This man will be a protector for you and your future family; he will provide for you and your future family; and he will pray for you and your future family. His sole desire will be to bring you to heaven and give you back to God, the only One who loves you more than he does.

As women, we often settle for less when it comes to men. We may do this for a variety of reasons. Maybe we do not know what type of person we want to spend our life with. Maybe we do not know ourselves. Maybe we do not know God and so we do not understand Love. Maybe we have been through a series of bad relationships and believe that we will only ever meet a certain type of man. Maybe we are impatient, and do not want to wait any longer to get married.

Whatever the reason may be, it is important during the closing days of this dating fast to focus on discovering God, yourself, and the attributes and qualities of the man God wants you to marry. Marriage is a sacrament. Like all sacraments it is instituted to provide the people receiving the sacrament with special graces. In addition, the sacrament of marriage is a vocation; it is a call to serve your spouse and future family. It is a covenant between God, man, and woman. When we make this lifelong commitment before God and our family and friends, God grants us His blessing and grace throughout the rest of our lives. Together the couple is a witness of Christ's love for His Church and the unbreakable bond between them. This is the type of man that God has chosen for you to marry. He will give you this man so long as you surrender your life to His love and patiently trust in His ways.

DARE: Write a letter to your future spouse about what you have discovered on this dating fast. What were your hopes and dreams going into the fast, and how have they evolved? Seal the letter, and save it to give to your future spouse the night before your wedding day. As well, start to pray for your future spouse. Pray that God will unite the two of you together and that you may be blessed with a long and joyous marriage.

Marriage leads to each other's sanctification

Matthew 1:18–25 "This is how the birth of Jesus came about. When his mother Mary was betrothed to Joseph, but before they lived together, she was found with child through the Holy Spirit. Joseph her husband, since he was a righteous man, yet unwilling to expose her to shame, decided to divorce her quietly. Such was his intention when, behold, the angel of the Lord appeared to him in a dream and said, 'Joseph, son of David, do not be afraid to take Mary your wife into your home. For it is through the Holy Spirit that this child has been conceived in her. She will bear a son and you are to name him Jesus, because he will save his people from their sins.' All this took place to fulfill what the Lord had said through the prophet: 'Behold, the virgin shall be with child and bear a son, and they shall name him Emmanuel,' which means 'God is with us.' When Joseph awoke, he did as the angel of the Lord had commanded him and took his wife into his home. He had no relations with her until she bore a son, and he named him Jesus."

Marriage is a sacrament of love that shows the incredible beauty of God's love here on earth and the beauty of love in this world. Therefore, marriage is a sacrament that involves three persons: man, woman, and God. The relationship between these three persons becomes one during the holy mass. Everything in each person's dating pasts is brought before God and placed on the altar. This is why marriage is a reflection of the Triune Godhead—God the Father, God the Son, and God the Holy Spirit. Marriage is a vocation that involves uncompromising love, unconditional acceptance, ceaseless dedication, total fidelity, and untiring service. These fruits are signs of God's love, and this is what makes Him present in the sacrament of matrimony. On your wedding day, you will both exclaim what Adam said about Eve: "This at last is bone of my bones and flesh of my flesh."

A positive and fruitful marriage is one where each spouse leads the other one closer to God, and if they are fortunate enough to be blessed with children, they teach their children the faith so that one day they can give the children back to God. How are you going to sanctify yourself during this fast in order to help sanctify your future husband and children? Remember that you cannot give something you do not have. This is especially true about love. Therefore, you must gain a deeper understanding and more intimate relationship with God before you share that love with others. In addition, a deeper understanding of the sacrament of marriage and genuine agape Love is needed before you fully enter into the marriage vocation. Remember that *you* are responsible for your future spouse's and children's path to eternal salvation. You must be adequately prepared in order to accept and carry out this call from God.

St. Joseph is a perfect example of how we are called to sanctify our spouse and children. Joseph was a righteous man who listened to God and protected both Mary and the baby Jesus. He trusted in the Lord and committed his life to serving his family. Although Joseph is often a silent player in the story of Christ, his role is extremely important. We are all called to follow St. Joseph's example in order to serve and sanctify our own families. Just as Joseph raised Jesus to give him back to God, so too we must raise our own children to eventually give them back to God.

DARE: Read the Bible passage about St. Joseph and reflect on how St. Joseph acted towards Mary and Jesus. What was his role in the life of Jesus and Mary? God wants each woman to find her St. Joseph here on earth to lead her to heaven. Write about the type of man you think God is calling you into marriage with. What attributes or characteristics should he embody? Why?

The Characteristics of
My Future Spouse

_____

_____

_____

_____

_____

_____

_____

_____

_____

_____

_____

_____

_____

_____

_____

_____

_____

_____

_____

_____

The Holy Sacrifice of the Mass

Galatians 5:22 "But when the Holy Spirit controls our lives He will produce this kind of fruit in us: love, joy, peace, patience, kindness, goodness, faithfulness, gentleness, and self-control."

This is the final day of the fast. Before you continue reading, pause for a moment and reflect on the fast. What have you experienced? How have you grown? How have you healed? Most importantly, what have you learned about yourself and your relationship with God?

If I told you that you could experience heaven on earth, would you want to partake in the event or not? Of course you would. We *can* experience heaven on earth – in fact, daily, if we take the time to do it. You may wonder how and where you can get such a glimpse of heaven. The answer is the Holy Sacrifice of the Mass. Every day at every hour somewhere in the world, Mass is being celebrated. As Catholics, we believe that when the priest consecrates the host and blesses the wine, Jesus descends onto the altar and becomes visibly present to us. It is during the consecration that the bread and wine become His body and blood. It is the most real and tangible form of Jesus that we can receive on earth. If you ever need or desire to visibly see Christ, attend the Holy Mass, and He will physically reveal Himself to you on the altar.

The physical act of the consecration of the body and blood is not the only part of the Mass that tells us that we experience heaven every time we go to Mass. The Eucharistic prayers said by the priest during the consecration reveal that in addition to Jesus being present to us, so too are all of the angels and saints in heaven. They, too, are physically present in the church as we kneel before Christ's body and blood. Each of the Eucharistic prayers said by the priest confirms this heavenly presence. Eucharist Prayer I states, "For ourselves, too, we ask some share in the fellowship of your apostles and martyrs, with John the Baptist, Stephen, Matthias, Barnabas, (names of other Saints) and all the saints." Similarly, Eucharist Prayer II reads, "Have mercy on us all; make us worthy to share eternal life with Mary, the virgin Mother of God, with the apostles, and with all the saints who have done your will throughout the ages. May we praise you in union with them, and give you glory through your Son, Jesus Christ." These are two of the four prayers a priest may say when consecrating the bread and wine.

Regardless of the specific prayer being offered, they point to the same bold claim: we are in union with all of the angels and saints at the time of the consecration of the body and blood of Christ. We all kneel before the altar of the Lord. At this moment of the Mass (two times), heaven is touching down on earth as we pray, and all of the angels and saints pray in union with us. If you stop and reflect on the actions and prayers being offered at this point in the Mass, you will experience tremendous comfort and peace. The phrase "the body of Christ" is more than just a metaphor. We truly are all part of the body of Christ, whether we are here on earth or reside in heaven.

DARE: Go to Mass and offer up praise and thanksgiving for everything that you have discovered on this dating fast. Make a commitment to continue to let the Holy Spirit lead you throughout your life. Journal about your personal growth and healing over this time period. You will not be 100% healed—after all, this fast was only for 40 days, and our journey with Christ is a lifelong commitment. Still, think about what you have learned, how you plan to act differently based on this fasting experience, and how you plan to enter into more fruitful relationships with others, especially men whom you date. Your mind and heart should be more focused on Christ, so be patient and let Him lead you to your future spouse and the one who will eventually bring you to God so you may rest in eternal happiness with Our Father.

What Happens Next?

Now that 40 days have passed and the dating fast is over, who are you going to be on day 102, 547, or 12,009? Just because the fast has ended does not mean that you should return to life as usual. If you have followed the meditations and actions for every day, daring to love Christ and yourself more fully, you are beginning to grow out of your old ways and have less desire to return to them. Return to the actions of each day and use them for daily spiritual progress as you move forward. Decide today on which actions you want to make part of your daily life. Can you set aside 10 minutes of silence every morning to listen for Christ's instruction? Can you continue to make yourself available to others through random acts of kindness or service so that you learn more about how to give of yourself?

As important as the dating fast is, completing it does not mean that you now have a spouse waiting for you on your doorstep. That is not how God operates, and this fast should remind you that all things come to fruition in His time, not yours. Be patient and continue to trust in His ways. When approached with prayer and love for Christ, the journey to marriage can be just as important and meaningful as the destination itself, so remain hopeful and know that everything works out in the end.

Regardless of where your life leads you, your heart must always reside in Christ, even when you get married and have children. His love will perfect your love for them and show you how to be the best wife and mother. The graces that you obtained on this fast will abundantly flow onto your spouse and children, even when you are not aware of it. If you continue to wait to carry out the vocation of marriage, may the memories and graces from the fast serve as a gentle reminder of Christ's presence in your life and provide you with hope and trust for your future, whatever it may entail. He will lead you to the one He has chosen for you. Whatever your situation in life, God continues to shower you with His blessings and love. His grace leaves you with a peace that makes your heart smile. Strive for virtue every day of your life so you can grow closer to God. Love Him first, and let His love pour out onto all of your relationships with other people.

Life is a road to be built, not a path to be followed. It is made with bricks of love, care, wisdom, and knowledge. Along the way are bridges of patience and understanding. You build the road every day with the choices you make and the sacrifices you offer. Obstacles sometimes arise, and you must decide whether to drive through them or steer around them. You will run into others on this road as well — some who are traveling to the same destination, and some who wish only to destroy the road you have already made. Remember that the road is short. Work hard, and pray even harder.

How to Pray the Rosary
"The Mysteries and Events in the Life of Jesus"

The rosary is comprised of a series of prayers that are used to meditate on and contemplate the life, death, and resurrection of Jesus Christ. The rosary starts with the Apostle's Creed, which is said on the Crucifix. After the Creed, you say an Our Father, 3 Hail Mary's, and a Glory Be.

After the introductory prayers, you will recite 5 *decades*, each comprised of an Our Father, 10 Hail Mary's, and a Glory Be. After each Glory Be, before starting the next decade with an Our Father, recite the Prayer to Jesus requested by Our Lady.

After you complete the 5 decades, recite the Hail Holy Queen and Prayer After the Rosary.

Prayer Before the Rosary

Queen of the Holy Rosary, you have deigned to come to Fatima to reveal to the three shepherd children the treasures of grace hidden in the Rosary. Inspire my heart with a sincere love of this devotion, in order that by meditating on the Mysteries of our Redemption which are recalled in it, I may obtain peace for the world, the conversion of sinners, and the favor which I ask of you in this Rosary (Mention your prayer requests). I ask this for the greater glory of God, for your own honor, and for the good of souls, especially for my own. Amen.

In the Name of the Father, the Son, and the Holy Spirit, Amen.

The Apostles Creed

I believe in God, the Father Almighty, Creator of Heaven and earth; and in Jesus Christ His only Son, Our Lord; who was conceived by the Holy Spirit, born of the Virgin Mary, suffered under Pontius Pilate, was crucified, died and was buried. He descended into Hell; the third day He arose again from the dead; He ascended into Heaven, and is seated at the right hand of God, the Father Almighty; from thence He shall come to judge the living and the dead. I believe in the Holy Spirit, the Holy Catholic Church, the communion of Saints, the forgiveness of sins, the resurrection of the body, and life everlasting. Amen.

Our Father

Our Father who art in heaven, hallowed be Thy name; Thy kingdom come; Thy will be done on earth as it is in Heaven. Give us this day our daily bread; and forgive us our trespasses as we forgive those who trespass against us; and lead us not into temptation, but deliver us from evil. Amen.

Hail Mary

Hail Mary, full of grace! The Lord is with thee; blessed art thou among women, and blessed is the fruit of thy womb, Jesus. Holy Mary, Mother of God, pray for us sinners now and at the hour of our death. Amen.

Glory Be to the Father

Glory be to the Father, and to the Son, and to the Holy Spirit. As it was in the beginning, is now, and ever shall be, world without end. Amen.

Prayer to Jesus Requested by Our Lady

O My Jesus, forgive us our sins, save us from the fires of hell, lead all souls to Heaven, especially those in most need of Thine mercy.

Hail Holy Queen

Hail Holy Queen, Mother of Mercy, our life, our sweetness and our hope. To you do we cry, poor banished children of Eve. To you do we send up our sighs, mourning and weeping in this valley of tears. Turn then, O most gracious advocate, your eyes of mercy toward us; and after this our exile show unto us the blessed fruit of your womb, Jesus. O clement! O loving! O sweet Virgin Mary! Pray for us, O Holy Mother of God, that we may be made worthy of the promises of Christ.

Prayer after the Rosary

O God, whose only-begotten Son, by His life, death and resurrection, has purchased for us the rewards of eternal life; grant, we beseech Thee, that, meditating upon these mysteries of the Most Holy Rosary of the Blessed Virgin Mary, we may imitate what they contain and obtain what they promise, through the same Christ our Lord. Amen.

In the Name of the Father, the Son, and the Holy Spirit, Amen.

About the Author

Katherine Becker is a doctoral student at the University of Wisconsin-Milwaukee, studying Interpersonal and Health Communication. Originally from Iowa, she received her B.A. and M.A. degrees in Communication from the University of Illinois at Urbana-Champaign. She spent two years as a research and evaluation contractor for the Centers for Disease Control & Prevention in Atlanta, Georgia. It was during her time in Atlanta that Katherine went on her first dating fast and began writing this book. She currently resides in Milwaukee, Wisconsin.